HONDA

CROWOOD MOTOCLASSICS

HONDA

The Complete Story

ROLAND BROWN

The Crowood Press

First published in 1991 by
The Crowood Press Ltd
Ramsbury, Marlborough
Wiltshire SN8 2HR

Paperback edition 1998

British Cataloguing in Publication Data

Brown, Roland
Honda.
1. Honda motorcycles, history
I. Title
629.2275

ISBN 1 86126 148 9

Typeset by Keyboard Services, Luton, Beds
Printed in Great Britain by
Butler & Tanner Ltd, Frome

Contents

HONDA HIGHLIGHTS

1906   Soichiro Honda born.

1910   Takeo Fujisawa born.

1922   Honda leaves his home village of Komyo to become auto apprentice in Tokyo, aged fifteen.

1936   Soichiro is injured in car-racing crash.

1937   Honda founds Tokai Seiki Heavy Industry Co. He finally succeeds in making piston ring.

1939   Fujisawa founds Japan Machine and Tool Research Institute.

1941   Japan enters Second World War at Pearl Harbour.

1945   Japan surrenders after atomic bombs dropped; Honda sells Tokai Seiki to Toyota for 450,000 yen.

1946   Soichiro sets up Honda Technical Research Institute in Hamamatsu.

1947   Kiyoshi Kawashima, who became President in 1973, joins company. Production of A-type two-stroke engine commences.

1948   Honda Motor Co. Ltd established in Hamamatsu with capital of one million yen.

1949   Production of 98cc D-type two-stroke Dream bike begins. Fujisawa joins Honda Motor Co.

1950   Tokyo branch of company is established.

1951   Four-stroke 146cc Dream E-type launched after recording 45mph (72kph) in tests.

1954   Honda enters a bike in race in Brazil, and announces plan to contest Isle of Man TT. Production of the Juno, Honda's first scooter.

1955   Company takes lead in Japanese bike production. Launch of the 250 and 350cc Dreams.

1958   Launch of the world's first step-thru motorbike, the 50cc C100 Super Cub.

1959   Company competes in TT for first time, finishing sixth in 125cc race. American Honda Motor Co. Inc. established.

1960   CB72, the sporty 250 which eventually became a popular export bike, launched in Japan.

1961   Mike Hailwood wins 250 and 125cc TTs on his way to 250 championship; Australian Tom Phillis wins 125cc world title for Honda. Monthly sales figures reach 100,000 bikes – an industry record.

1962   Honda sets up plant in Belgium to assemble and sell mopeds. Jim Redman (250 and 350cc) and Luigi Taveri (125cc) win world championships as Honda begins domination of smaller GP classes.

HONDA HIGHLIGHTS

1963   Company's first four-wheeler launched – the T360 pick-up truck. The S500, a 90mph (145kph) 500cc sports car, follows two months later.

1965   Honda UK Ltd established in London as company's annual sales reach one billion yen.
American Richie Ginther wins Mexican GP, less than two years after Honda's debut in Formula One.

1967   Super Cub sales pass the five million mark.

1968   Honda announces withdrawal from bike GPs after Mike Hailwood wins 250 and 350cc championships, but just misses 500cc crown.

1969   CB750 four launched: 'the first superbike'.

1971   Arrival of the first CB500 four.

1972   Civic 1200 car launched.

1973   President Soichiro Honda and Executive Vice-President Takeo Fujisawa retire; Kiyoshi Kawashima takes over as President.

1974   GL1000 Gold Wing launched.

1979   Four-stroke NR500 makes disastrous debut in Honda's return to GP road racing at Silverstone. Graham Noyce wins Honda's first 500cc motocross world championship.
Production commences at American plant in Maryville, Ohio.

1981   Honda's first turbocharged bike, the CX500 Turbo, launched.

1982   VF750S launched – the company's first V4.

1983   Freddie Spencer wins Honda's first 500cc road race title at San Marino GP, Imola.
Tadashi Kume succeeds Kawashima as President.

1985   Spencer wins the Swedish 500cc GP to clinch the double of 250 and 500cc world titles.

1986   Hondas finish in first, second, third, fifth and sixth places in the Paris–Dakar Rally.

1987   Honda-engined cars take the first four places in the British GP at Silverstone. Nigel Mansell wins in a Williams.
Production of the fifty-millionth Honda motorcycle to be built in Japan.

1988   Company's Japanese car production reaches fifteen million units.
Ayrton Senna wins F1 world championship in McLaren Honda, adding to the manufacturers' title won earlier in season.

1989   Honda Motor Co. Ltd produces 3,032,000 bikes, 1,903,000 cars and 1,543,000 'power products'. Net sales total US$26,433 million, of which 70.5 per cent is from automobiles, 10.1 per cent from motorcycles.
The oval-pistoned NR750 prototype takes the limelight at the Tokyo Show, and stars again at the Cologne Show in 1990.

Preface

Honda's contribution to motorcycling is probably best appreciated if you imagine for a moment what the world would be like without the biggest bike firm of all. Say Soichiro Honda's big car crash in 1936 had been more serious than it was; or he had had never met Takeo Fujisawa and put the Honda Motor Co. on the road to prosperity all those years ago. What then?

We'd still have bikes, of course, and no doubt many of them would still be fast and reliable and fun. But motorcycling wouldn't be the same, and not just because all the machines in this book would not exist.

Honda have been the biggest bike builders for years; but, more than that, they have been the pioneers, the leaders, the firm that everyone else has tried to shoot down. Honda put the world on two wheels with the Super Cub; Honda led the Japanese invasion that took motorcycling into a new era with a fresh image. The CB750 was labelled the first superbike but many more of the machines in the following pages were pretty super too. Motorcyclists owe a lot to Soichiro and Co. – even those whose T-shirts claim they would rather eat worms than ride a Honda.

Cramming more than thirty years of growth and achievement into one book has not been easy, and there are bound to be gaps. That is particularly true of the many models that were sold in some countries but not in others. Despite restricting coverage of later varieties mostly to British-spec bikes, there was nowhere near enough room for them all, but the more important ones are here.

Acknowledgements

I would like to thank the many people who have helped me invaluably in compiling this book. Kermit Whitfield sent many facts and photos from Honda in Tokyo. Graham Blunden was hugely informative and also dragged out his precious collection of bikes for a photo-call. Fellow VJMC members Don Leeson and Dave Jupp passed on some of their knowledge, as did Dave Barton from the Honda Owners' Club. Roly and Sally-Anne Batchelor and Dave Horner shared their enthusiasm for Gold Wings, as did Pete Broad and Clint Hooper theirs for CBXs.

Photographs came from a distinguished line-up of snappers: Jack Burnicle, Kel Edge, David Goldman, Patrick Gosling, Phil Masters, Don Morley, John Nutting and Tony Sleep. Dawn Lemon and June Buck of Rothmans raided files for precious pics, as did Bill Russell of Castrol, Sylviane Loyet of ELF and Lynn Reekes of Honda UK.

1

Early Days

From Army Surplus Engines
to the Super Cub

Tokyo, August 1949. Four years after the end of the Second World War the once-proud Imperial power of Japan was still struggling to its feet, its people trying to rebuild their lives and their cities and to understand how what they had believed to be their divine nation had been defeated.

Huge numbers of the capital's wooden houses had been destroyed by Allied fire-bombing in the final months of the War. The population was suffering from a severe lack of food and an economy dominated by black-market racketeers. American occupation troops were a common sight on the streets. Only in the few turbulent years since the surrender had Emperor Hirohito finally renounced his own divinity, women become entitled to vote, farmers been allowed to own land, and Japan begun to adopt a Western-type democracy.

The economic explosion that would soon hit Japan was certainly not a subject for small talk when Soichiro Honda hosted a party at his Hamamatsu headquarters, 150 miles (240km) south-west along the coast from Tokyo, to celebrate the creation of the first motorbike that his company had made all by themselves.

The desks were pushed into a corner, the story goes, so that President Honda and his twenty employees could eat sardines and pickles, and toast their 98cc two-stroke prototype with cups of home-brewed sake.

'It's like a dream,' someone said – and Honda immediately seized on the word for the name of his new bike. The little machine which until that moment had been known simply as the D-Type, with its single bicycle-style saddle, telescopic forks but no rear suspension, and its two-speed 3bhp engine held in a heavy-looking triangular frame, became the first Honda Dream.

Today the phrase Honda Dream still brings to mind humble bikes, albeit models such as the CB400N Dream which have six valves, two cylinders and top speeds of over 100mph (160kph). These days, the more impressive Honda two-wheelers have four or even six cylinders, oval pistons, on-board computers, components made from titanium and carbon fibre, and/or the ability to reach 180mph (290kph). It would have taken an imaginative dream for Soichiro to have envisaged much of that even in his sleep, just over forty years ago.

The firm he created is by far the world's largest motorcycle manufacturer, every day adding thousands of

---

Soichiro Honda: Mechanic of the Century

The eldest son of a poor Hamamatsu blacksmith, Soichiro Honda rose to become head of one of the world's leading industrial groups. But while his partner Fujisawa took care of the money, Honda was by nature more artisan than businessman.

His fascination with machinery started early. Born in November 1906, as a child Soichiro helped his father repair bicycles. Boyhood interest in a local rice mill's rarity of a petrol engine – cars were scarce in Japan in the 1920s – was followed by an apprenticeship at a motor repair shop in Tokyo.

Honda used the evenings to build his own racing car round an ex-military V8 Curtis-Wright aircraft engine, winning numerous races in it, and continued to build racing cars after returning to Hamamatsu to start up his own branch of the repair shop.

Predictably, he modified his cars, tuning one Ford motor with a supercharger, and reportedly even tilting the engine to help in the predominantly left-hand bends. But he hurt himself badly in the 1936 All-Japan Speed Rally near Tokyo, breaking several bones and injuring his face on colliding with a car being driven out of the pits.

The next year Honda changed direction, setting up a firm called Tokai Seiki Heavy Industry Co. to manufacture piston rings. *

His first rings were brittle and useless but eventually, after having one analysed by a local professor, Soichiro discovered that the problem was lack of silicone. He realized how little he knew and became a part-time student, soon afterwards producing his first usable piston ring.

Business was good and, after Japan had become involved in the war, Honda found big customers such as Toyota, the navy and aviation companies. He gained more favour with the military by designing machinery that dramatically speeded up production of aeroplanes' wooden propellors.

The Hamamatsu factory was damaged by bombing towards the end of the war, and after the surrender Honda decided to start afresh. He sold out to Toyota for a small fortune, then took a year off to make his own whisky, party with friends and play musical instruments. Soichiro Honda's real life's work was about to commence.

*In Tetsuo Sakaya's excellent book *Honda: The Men, the Management, the Machines*, from which many early details in this book have been taken.

Soichiro Honda as a young man.

bikes to a production total that stands at well over fifty million. Honda have moved into four-wheeled production with such success that the company now ranks as one of the leading car makers, too, and supplied the engines which in recent seasons have made the Formula One world-championship-winning McLaren race team so dominant.

But it was by dealing in engines for little motorbikes that Soichiro Honda began, after setting up what he called the Honda Technical Research Institute in a small wooden shed in Hamamatsu in October 1946. If the title sounds a little pretentious, perhaps it's an indication that all along Soichiro really did have dreams of conquering the world. Even then, at the age of thirty-nine, he had already experienced success as a businessman, spending the war years building up a piston-ring and propellor-making firm that he then sold to Toyota.

Having been fascinated by vehicles of one sort or another since his schooldays, Honda then saw that the combination of Japan's feeble post-war economy and the country's over-crowded public transport system left scope for a machine that could give people mobility at a cheap price. He bought up a batch of small-capacity army-surplus engines and fixed them to bicycles, using a belt to drive the back wheel.

The resultant contraption could barely be called a motor-bike. Photographs from those earliest days show exactly what you might expect from its list of components: bicycle handlebars, a narrow bicycle saddle and bicycle tyres, and a small two-stroke motor bolted to the downtube of its reinforced diamond-type bicycle frame.

The motor was reckoned to produce about one horse-

Twenty-eight years on from Honda's beginnings in 1946, the CB750, launched in 1968, remained in much the same form right up until 1976.

power, and it was a rather lazy horse at that. The bike often required many minutes of frantic pedaling before it would splutter into life, and needed human assistance when faced by the gentlest of hills. But it was better than cycling – just. Soichiro sold all he could build, and made a handy profit.

Turpentine Oil: Honda's Home Brew

At the same time, with petrol heavily rationed and hard to find, he came up with a plan to produce turpentine oil, which Japan's military had unsuccessfully attempted to use to power fighter planes several years earlier. The oil came from the roots of pine trees, so Honda bought a pine forest and set to work with dynamite to blast out some roots. Unfortunately, this was one of his less successful enterprises. His inexperienced pyrotechnics triggered a fire which burned down most of his trees.

The experience was not completely wasted, though. Although Honda was able to obtain petrol on the black market, this sometimes led to problems when the police asked where it had come from. But adding turpentine oil – which Soichiro eventually managed to produce – to the petrol, resulted in a mixture that smelled of pine and burned with a cloud of pungent smoke from the exhaust. The authorities, it seems, were easily convinced that the fuel was merely turpentine oil and thus outside their control.

Soichiro's next problem was that supplies of the ex-army motors soon ran out. After the war he had not been the only one to hit on the idea of providing transport for the masses.

Other small businesses with names such as Fuji, Pointer, Showa, Sanyo and Rocket produced similar motorbikes from a combination of bought-in engines and bicycle chassis. Many used generator motors made by the Tohatsu company; it's likely that Honda was one of them.

But after a while Tohatsu realized that they would be better off producing the little bikes themselves, and supplies of the motors to the other firms rapidly dried up. This was less of a problem for Honda, with his varied mechanical background and experience of piston-ring design, than to others. Soichiro decided to design his own engine instead and it turned out, not surprisingly, to be a fairly exact copy of the Tohatsu: a 50cc two-stroke with vertical cylinder, single speed, belt drive to the rear wheel, magneto ignition and a slide carburettor.

Like the military motor, Honda's version made a maximum of about 1bhp at 5,000rpm. A thin exhaust pipe ran down from the front of the engine, heading left towards a silencer near the rear wheel when the powerplant was bolted into the normal suspensionless pushbike frame. On the crossbar sat a small petrol tank, its turpentine-based contents earning the motor its less-than-generous nickname The Chimney.

The finished machine was the Honda Model A, and a 1947 photograph (reprinted in a 1973 advertisement with the catchline 'Honda didn't always have more motorcycles. A quarter century ago we started with one') shows a proud Soichiro in cap, tie and white coat, standing alongside his baby outside the shed-like Honda Technical Research Institute building in which it had been designed and built.

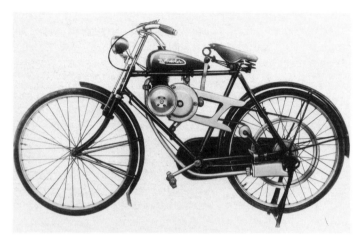

The Model A of 1947 was little more than a Honda-designed, 1bhp engine in a modified pushbike chassis.

The Model A Honda was undoubtedly crude and less than exciting to ride, but it was cheap and it worked – eventually. Not surprisingly, it went down very well in post-war Japan, but Soichiro did not leave his bike alone for long. Within a few months he had found supplies of a better chassis, still along pushbike lines but with a stronger, lower, triangular-shaped frame which looked a little more like something suited to a motorcycle.

The wheels and tyres were sturdier, too. Tiny cable-operated drum brakes replaced the cycle-style blocks, and there was even suspension of sorts. At the front, spindly girder forks pivoted on a joint beneath the steering head.

The top end of the forks moved against a small horizontal spring in front of the handlebar stem. Rear suspension was limited to large springs supporting the saddle, but the bike was a distinct improvement.

The next year, 1948, Soichiro renamed the Honda Technical Research Institute simply the Honda Motor Co. Ltd, and diversified into three wheels. He enlarged the Model A's motor to 90cc, turned it round and bolted it to a delivery-bike chassis – basically a modified bicycle frame with two rear wheels and a big box in between. The Model B, as the trike was imaginatively called, had a revised front suspension comprising vertically-sprung girder forks, and also gained a headlamp.

The capacity increase gave only a fraction more power but later that year Honda brought out his Model C solo, with its output uprated to about 3bhp at 3000rpm. This used much the same frame as the later A-models, with B-type forks and a bicycle-type carrier above the back wheel, but was basically similar in appearance.

These first three machines had used Honda's engines in bought-in chassis, some made by a firm called Kitagawa, but the next big step was not far away. By August of the next year the first wholly Honda motorcycle was complete, and Soichiro's Dream was metal and rubber.

The Model D was a much chunkier device than Honda's previous efforts, with a thick pressed-steel frame formed from two large triangular sections placed side by side. The petrol tank – no nasty turpentine needed by now, it seems – was set into the frame, which initially had no rear suspension but used telescopic forks, Honda's first, at the front.

The motor was another two-stroke single, its 98cc capacity coming from 50 × 50mm bore and stroke dimensions. Although the Dream made only a horsepower it dispensed with pedals, instead being fired up by a kickstarter on the right. On the other side, a rocking foot pedal worked the two-speed gearbox, the output of which reached the rear wheel via an efficiently guarded final-drive chain.

Opposites Attract: The Arrival of Fujisawa

The Dream was the first complete motorcycle to be built by one company since the war. This was a milestone in the history of Honda, and even that of the country. However, it could be argued that the most significant event in the history of the Honda Motor Company was not the launch of the stocky Model D, but a meeting that took place in the same month. For it was also in August 1949 that Soichiro Honda was first introduced by a mutual friend to Takeo Fujisawa, the man who would play such a vital role in the firm's success.

Only three years after it had been founded, Honda was already a thriving business employing twenty people. New premises had been added in Hamamatsu in 1948 and the future looked good. But Soichiro needed money to help him invest. Most of all, the engineer, who loved getting his hands dirty, needed someone to sell the bikes he produced.

Fujisawa was that man. When they met Fujisawa was thirty-eight, Honda forty-two. They immediately got on

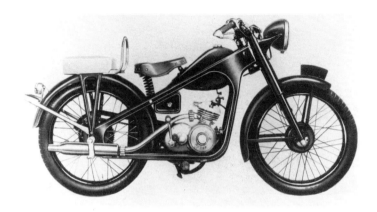

The first Dream, the 98cc two-stroke Model D of 1949, was the first bike that Honda and his twenty employees built all by themselves.

well and decided to go into business together, seemingly realizing that between them they had the potential for big things.

Fujisawa made his presence felt almost immediately by reorganizing the company's distribution set-up. At the time of the Dream's launch Honda were selling the 98cc engine on its own, to be put into frames made by Kitagawa. This made Honda vulnerable when the frame company dramatically cut production from the normal figure of about 100 units a month.

The surplus engines hit demand for Honda's products and, while Soichiro apparently thought that the best solution was to help Kitagawa, Fujisawa was a little more ruthless. He told distributors that if they wanted to sell the new Dream they couldn't also continue to buy engines or deal with the frame company.

Many dealers did not like the new approach; a few disliked it enough to threaten Fujisawa with knives. (These days, some sectors of the motorcycle trade are less inclined to violence.) But, although some distributors were lost, others were found to take their place and the number of Honda dealers gradually increased to about forty.

The Dream was a competent, sturdily built bike but was not outstandingly popular, partly because in winter its big, close-fitting mudguards would often get clogged with mud on Japan's rough roads. Another problem, Fujisawa told Honda, was that people preferred rival firms' four-stroke exhaust notes to the Dream's high-pitched two-stroke scream. Soichiro's answer came in 1951 with the Model E, the company's first four-stroke, and he apparently came to share the sentiment. In later years the company would favour four-strokes almost completely.

The Model E's engine was Honda's biggest by far, a 146cc single with three overhead valves – two inlet, one

---

Takeo Fujisawa: Man Who Made the Money

Designing and building good machines are all very well, but to a motorcycle manufacturer the most important thing of all is to *sell* them, and to make a profit in doing so. As the financial genius behind the Honda Motor Co. from 1949 to his retirement in 1973, Takeo Fujisawa was arguably as vital as Soichiro Honda himself to the firm's success.

All through the two men's long partnership, while Honda came up with the hardware it was Fujisawa who handled the money and the marketing – raising capital, organizing distributors and the ever-growing labour force, setting up exports, controlling investments. The combination of his and Honda's very different skills allowed each to pursue the things he was good at.

Fujisawa was born in 1910, four years after Honda, and spent most of his childhood in poverty after his father's business had been wrecked by recession and the huge Tokyo earthquake of 1923. Lack of education led to menial work and a brief spell in the army before Takeo landed a job in a steel merchant's, where his skill as a salesman soon began to show.

He rose through the ranks there, taking over as manager when the steel firm's owner was enlisted to fight in the war with China, and then left to set up a successful business based round supplying tools to the military.

After the end of the Second World War he came to Tokyo looking for a new business to get involved in, and heard from a friend about the 'brilliant young inventor', Soichiro Honda, who was looking for a backer. They met and immediately decided to team up, and Fujisawa joined the three-year-old Honda company in October 1949.

When Executive Vice-President Takeo Fujisawa retired twenty-four years later, on the same day as Soichiro himself, the company's capital value had increased from two million yen to 19.48 *billion*. The man who looked after Honda's finance had done a pretty good job.

exhaust, like modern Dreams – worked via pushrods running up the back of the cylinder barrel from a camshaft at the top of the crankcase. Output was about 5bhp at 5,000rpm.

Like the Model D stroker, the E had a two-speed gearbox and chain final drive. Its chassis was almost identical, too, but performance was much better, as Honda and Fujisawa discovered when they tested the prototype in the Hakone mountains that summer.

Kiyoshi Kawashima, who had helped Soichiro with the bike's design (and would become President twenty-two years later on Honda's retirement), set off on the Model E in pouring rain, with the other two following in a Buick car. As the gradient steepened, Kawashima left the Buick far behind. Even today, the Honda Motor Co.'s official note of the incident lists proudly that 'Dream E-type motorcycle undergoes test riding at Hakone and records average speed of 70kph [43mph]'.

The bike was launched that October and, although it burned oil and didn't handle particularly well – the rear end was converted from rigid to plunger suspension on later models – the four-stroke sold well. Production of the E displaced the Model D in Honda's new Tokyo plant, and the new bike's output of 130 units a day set a Japanese record.

Honda's next move was to go back to basics. Although Japan's economy was slowly recovering in the early 1950s, many people were still poor and could not afford a 'proper' motorbike. The Honda Model F was aimed at the masses and echoed the company's very earliest attempts, being basically a 50cc two-stroke engine fitted to a standard bicycle.

The F was much more sophisticated than the Model A of five years earlier. The little 1bhp motor was designed so that it could quickly be clipped alongside the pushbike's back wheel, and connected up by chain. A round petrol tank was bolted to the bike frame below the saddle, the whole lot weighing only about 15lb (7kg) and looking respectably neat.

The idea and execution of the Cub, as the Model F was called, were good, but more crucial was Fujisawa's approach to selling it. At that time Japan had only a few hundred

The Model F of 1952 was a 50cc two-stroke engine designed to be clipped to a bicycle frame. By the end of the year Honda was building 7,000 a month.

Honda's Saitama plant was completed in 1953, the same year that the fast-growing company's headquarters moved from Hamamatsu to Tokyo.

motorcycle dealers but more than ten times as many bicycle agents. Fujisawa wrote to almost all of them, telling them about the Cub, and was immediately deluged with 30,000 replies, enabling him to set up a distribution network of 13,000 dealers almost overnight.

By now, the Honda Motor Co. Ltd was growing at an incredible rate. In October 1952 they began exporting the Dream to the Philippines (the Cub was already being sold in Taiwan); the next month Soichiro went to America to check out their production methods and to order a million dollars' worth of machine tools. In the month after that Honda produced 7,000 Cubs, which was 70 per cent of the total Japanese bike output. By December 1953, a year later, several big new plants had been opened and the company's capital was rated at sixty million yen.

Catching up with Convenience: The Model J. Benly

Honda had also come up with what was arguably their first bike that could stand comparison with Europe – the Model J, or Benly. The first of a long line of models with that name, which means 'convenience' or 'economy' in Japanese, the 1953 Benly was a 90cc four-stroke single whose design was copied unashamedly from a West German NSU.

The pushrod motor made about 4bhp at 6,000rpm and had a three-speed gearbox, but more important was the chassis, which with its pressed-steel frame and tidier detailing had a much more modern look. Forks were telescopic, complete with little gaiters at the bottom, and the bike had a peculiar rear suspension which involved both engine and swing arm moving round a central pivot.

The Benly was followed at the beginning of the next year by the Juno, Honda's first scooter, which again followed current European thinking in its styling. Soichiro's version used a 200cc four-stroke single motor (later uprated to 219cc) with a three-speed gearbox. Following the fashion, the engine was positioned at the rear, beneath the seat, and the wheels were small. A rather complicated multi-section screen, faired-in indicators and a pillion seat with a grab-handle all gave the Juno a well equipped if slightly porky appearance.

At this point, early 1954, things were going brilliantly for the Honda Motor Co. In the previous four years the company's sales had increased at a staggering rate: from eighty-two million yen in the year to February 1951, to 330 the next year, then to 2,438, and finally to 7,729 million in the year to February 1954. In the same period profit had risen from four million to thirteen million, then to 100 million, then to 514 million yen.

Fujisawa's new policy of separate dealership networks for the Cub and bigger bikes, and demanding cash up front for the latter, was providing much money for reinvestment in machinery and labour. Profits up from four million yen to 514 million in three years! Where would it all end?

Civil War: Battle of the Japanese Bike Builders

If the Japanese motorcycle manufacturers' struggle for world dominance has often been bloody, then their fights for domestic supremacy have been no less fierce. The current total of four firms is a far cry from the pioneering days of the early 1950s, when Japan had scores of separate motorcycle producers.

The country's bike industry is estimated by some to date back as far as 1908, but before the Second World War the number of machines produced was always fairly small. In 1940, for example, the total output only just topped 3,000 bikes.

By no means were all of these the bicycle-type lightweights with which the industry was revitalized in the aftermath of the war. In the late 1930s some of the most popular machines were side-valve twins made by a firm called Rukuo, which produced copies of Harley-Davidson models under licence and carried on building the bikes, without worrying about the licence, after Japan unleashed war on the Americans at Pearl Harbour.

Meguro, founded in 1924, was one of the oldest Japanese firms. Their flagship before the war was a 500cc single which owed much of its design to Britain's Velocette. Later they also produced 500 and 650cc twins based on BSA's A7 series. (Whether the copies leaked oil as reliably is not known.) But, like the British firm themselves, Meguro suffered from lack of investment and forward thinking. By 1961 they were in decline, and were taken over by Kawasaki Heavy Industries when the shipbuilding giant sought a method of getting into the motorcycle business in a big way.

Before Honda took over in the mid-1950s it was Tohatsu, whose 50cc engines Soichiro probably used to power his first bikes, who were market leaders. Basing their production on small two-strokes such as the 60cc Puppy and later the 50cc Runpet, their 1955 output of over 70,000 bikes was more than double Honda's. But Tohatsu then went into decline, and in the early 1960s a lengthy strike put the firm out of business.

Bridgestone was the last major firm to disappear. In the 1950s they made two-stroke engines for other firms to use. Then came some innovative and quick two-stroke twins – notably the 90mph (145kph) 350 GTR – before the plug was pulled by the parent tyre company, for whom bikes were just a sideline, in 1968. Which left the Big Four . . .

The whole Honda story very nearly ended right there in 1954, because the company hit a series of disasters which very nearly caused its downfall. First, sales began to fall. The bicycle-based Cub was becoming too basic, the Benly was thought by many to be mechanically noisy, the Juno scooter's enclosed engine led to overheating, and the long-running Model E Dream, by now bored out from its original 146 to 225cc to give more power, was showing its limitations.

At the same time Japan was in a recession following the end of the Korean War in 1953. The unions were growing stronger and demanding higher wages, and Honda was heavily committed to a huge turnover based on previous figures. Although sales for the year ending February 1955 dropped by only 20 per cent, profit slumped from that magical 514 million yen to just sixty-eight million. With the future looking increasingly bleak, Fujisawa at one point even considered declaring the company bankrupt.

But with the co-operation of the Mitsubishi Bank; the subcontractors, many of whom were owed money; and the unions, who backed the company and worked round the clock to build and sell a special run of 200cc Dreams (improved by the fitment of a new carburettor), Honda came through.

Although it took a few years for the figures to approach previous levels, the company had been saved. And in one way, at least, the country's problems almost certainly helped Honda. The huge number of Japanese bike firms had gradually diminished throughout the decade and, around the time of Honda's problems, big rival Tohatsu closed down,

following a year-long strike. In September 1955 Honda took over the lead in domestic motorcycle production. They have been number one ever since.

The mid-1950s were a time of relative caution for Honda, but Soichiro did not hold back from developing new bikes. In the spring of 1955 the company launched two similar new models in a pattern that would be repeated in years to come – 250 and 350cc Dreams designated the SA and SB respectively.

These four-stroke singles were obvious derivatives of the earlier Benly but taken a stage further – bigger petrol tanks, the addition of front downtubes for the pressed-steel frames, beefy mudguards, twin rear shock units, headlamp nacelles, and fully enclosed drive chains. With their little winged-tank emblem – very similar to the one still used today – and the word 'Dream' impressed upon the bulbous sidepanels, these bikes gave the first real hint of what was to come.

But their main importance was as the first Hondas to use an overhead camshaft, driven by a chain running up the right side of the vertically positioned barrel. The new Dreams were bigger, faster and better than the bikes that had gone before, and overhead cam was without doubt the way to go.

Selling to the Nice People: The C100 Super Cub

There is not much doubt that of all the brilliant bikes Honda have built – the CB750 superbike, Mike Hailwood's magnifi-

The heavily-built 250cc four-stroke Dream SA arrived in 1955, the year that Honda took over from Tohatsu as leading Japanese motorcycle manufacturers.

cent six-cylinder racers, the mighty Gold Wing, you name them – the most important of all is the C100 Super Cub of 1958. Quite simply, this humble little 40mph (65kph) runabout changed the face of motorcycling, introducing bikes to people all over the world and providing Honda with the finance to produce so many infinitely more exciting things in the future.

Like all the best inventions, the Super Cub seems so

simple that anyone might have thought of it. As its name suggests, Soichiro's machine was a development of his attempt to put the world on two wheels with his cheap-and-cheerful motorized bicycle called the Cub. The Super Cub did just that by adding ease of use, reliability, cleanliness, weather protection and even a tiny taste of style to the Cub's original assets of simplicity, economy and convenience.

Others had tried and come close, and the post-war scooter boom had shown that small-capacity enclosed motorcycles could be popular. Honda's brainwave was to keep the full enclosure of scooters, including his own Juno, but to move the motor away from beneath the seat to a more conventional motorbike location between the rider's legs. This allowed both easier engine cooling and bigger wheels. The latter proved an advantage both physically, in their performance on poor roads, and mentally, in that to many people the similarity to the bicycle was attractive.

Once the concept had been finalized, Honda did not spoil it by trying to make the Super Cub *too* cheap. From the word go the bike had decent electrics hidden away in its pressed-steel frame, big mudguards, a reasonably well padded seat, and a fully enclosed drive chain. The C100's engine – rather confusingly a 50cc pushrod unit producing a claimed 4.5bhp at 9,500rpm – had three gears and an automatic clutch, and was kept out of sight behind the plastic legshield section.

To say that the Super Cub sold superbly well would be understating the obvious. Backed by inspired advertising – notably the 'You meet the nicest people on a Honda' line,

with its illustrations showing many different types of people enjoying the ride – it rapidly became the best-selling motorbike of all time. A new type of bike, the step-thru or scooterette, had arrived, and motorcycling in general benefited greatly.

The 'Nicest People' ad originated with the Grays agency in Los Angeles, appearing in publications like *Playboy* and general-interest magazines like *Life*, before transferring to television. It proved the key to huge export success for Honda in the States and elsewhere. The campaign was another landmark for Honda, for even the Super Cub had not sold when introduced alongside the Dream and Benly in American Honda's chain of motorcycle shops.

But as well as running the advertisements the US importers changed sales direction, offering the Super Cub to shops selling sports and leisure goods. The affluent American public, previously put off bikes by thoughts of noise, grease, Hell's Angels and films like *The Wild One*, lapped it up.

A huge new market had been born, and the States was just the start of Honda's export success. Sales networks were set up in Germany in 1961, in Belgium and Britain in 1962, in France in 1964. Over half a million Super Cubs were sold in almost every year from 1960 onwards, with a peak of nearly 900,000 three years later. At one stage they were popping off the production line at a rate of one every 12sec.

The original Super Cub spawned dozens of spin-offs over the years both from rivals and from Honda themselves, most of them too tedious to go into in detail here. In 1960

The legendary C100 Super Cub was introduced in 1958, and owed much of its early success to ads such as 'You meet the nicest people on a Honda'.

Soichiro Honda (left) and Takeo Fujisawa (right) retired together in October 1973.

alone there were the electric-start C102 Super Cub; the CZ100 monkey bike, with its similar engine but tiny balloon-tyred wheels; and the C110 Sports Cub, with a bit more power and later a four-speed gearbox too. In later years there were C70s, C90s and C-just-about-everything-in-betweens. The glorious ranks of Honda step-thrus and mopeds later included names such as the Port-Cub, the Chaly, the Naughty Dax and the Super Sports SS50 –

complete with disc brake, snappy styling and, in Britain at least, the pedals necessary to allow sixteen-year-olds to circumvent strange licensing laws.

But the one true classic was the Super Cub, the durability of its design proven by the simple fact that the C90 Cub, still Honda's best-selling bike in Britain in 1990, looks virtually identical to that first C100.

2

Take Two

Honda's Twins Are Born

The single-cylinder Dreams that Honda had built in the mid-1950s had been particularly inspired by German NSUs of the time, so nobody should have been too surprised when Soichiro's first twin, the C70, appeared in 1957 also owing much to NSU.

In fact the little twins wouldn't appear in Europe for several years, and even when they did many Western motorcyclists took little notice of them with their high-revving aluminium engines, pressed-steel frames and leading-link forks. When people did comment it was often to snigger that the Japanese buzz-bombs had no torque, didn't handle and wouldn't last.

If the cynics had an argument on the first two points, they couldn't have been more wrong on the third. Compared with British twins of the time, with their separate gearboxes, often leaky vertically split crankcases and general lack of sophistication, even the first Honda twins were well built and well equipped little machines.

The C70 starred a 250cc unit-construction motor (its four-speed gearbox all in one with the engine), with cylinders angled slightly forward. The crankshaft ran at 360 degrees, pistons rising and falling together, and a central chain drove the single overhead camshaft. Peak power was claimed to be 18bhp at 7,400rpm.

Like Honda's singles of the time it was a substantial and rather ungainly-looking cycle, with not only the frame but the forks being made of hefty pressings welded together. Big mudguards dwarfed 16in wheels; single-leading-shoe drum brakes attempted to bring the 350lb (160kg) bike to a halt; and for the rider there was a cantilever saddle with a rear carrier plus optional pad for a pillion.

The C70 came equipped with a mirror and indicators, by no means common at the time, and a year later its replacement, the C71, added an electric starter mounted in front of the crankcases. The passenger's lot improved with the dual seat fitted to the sportier CS71 option, which also boasted a couple of extra horsepower (20bhp at 4,800rpm) from increased compression, and a raised exhaust system.

What's in a Name?

Honda certainly extracted good mileage from the name Dream, after coining it at that 1949 sake party in celebration of the new Model D. The Honda Motor Co. was still producing bikes called Dreams several decades later and, although the majority of Hondas are not given names, several classic monikers have reappeared time and again over the years.

The first Cub was the Model F bicycle-with-an-engine of 1952, and the C90 step-thru was still being sold with that name in Britain in the 1990s. When the step-thru first appeared, in 1958, it was given the title Super Cub; over the years, the word Super has often been tagged on in an attempt to add glamour.

Another Honda favourite is Benly, a name which was first used for the 90cc Model J in 1953. In later years Benly came to suggest a plodding commuter twin, but Benlys had their moments. The best-known early Benly was the CB92, a racy little 125cc twin.

In the States in 1962 the 250cc CB72 roadster was sold as the Hawk, with the 305cc CB77 being called the Super Hawk.

Americans have tended to use names more than Europeans over the years – such decisions are normally left to importers and their marketing advisors – and the name Hawk cropped up right through to the 1990s, when it was used for a middleweight V-twin.

A slightly modified verson of that bike became the Revere in Britain, where names have generally been used sparingly. When the Yanks talked about their Hurricanes, for example, the Limeys discussed mere CBRs. Americans cruised on Interceptors and Sabres; Brits rode down-to-earth VFs and VFRs.

Perhaps Honda's most successful name of all was the one coined for the bike built for Americans but sold all over the world: the Gold Wing. Even people who knew nothing about motorcycles realized that the Gold Wing stood for flying with a first-class ticket.

In 1958 Honda also produced an off-road version of the 250, the RC70f, which had knobbly tyres on large-diameter wheels, no lights or electric starter, different frame and handlebars, and open pipes running high up the right of the bike. The three 250cc options were just the start of Honda's attempt to cover every corner of the market with numerous variations on a theme.

The twin-pot motor was also shrunk to 125cc to produce the C90, which put out 11.5bhp at 9,500rpm and was basically an all-round smaller version of the C70. This in turn spawned the CB90, the CB prefix indicating sporty pretentions which were backed up by the spec: humpy petrol tank, smaller dual seat and mudguards, flyscreen on top of the headlamp shell, and twin-leading-shoe front drum brake.

Then there were the slightly bigger models, the C95 and sportier CB95, which copied the features of the 125s but whose engines were bored out to 154cc for a little extra power. And a similar thing happened to the 250s, which were bored out to 305cc to produce the base-model C75 and the sportier CS76.

This pattern of proliferation in various sizes and types would carry on throughout the early 1960s, with the range seemingly increasing all the time until even Honda must have had a tough job keeping track of all the various models. But it was the sportier CB-series bikes that made the company's name in the export market.

The 125cc CB92 was first seen in 1959 along with its dowdier brother the C92, and made a fairly favourable impact when it hit Europe a couple of years later. True, the handling was nothing to write home about, and the combination of pressed-steel frame and underdamped suspension caused a few interesting moments.

But the little bike was a flyer, whirring up to 60mph (97kph)-plus once you got used to keeping its high-revving little motor spinning fast, and Honda's attention to detail won them many admirers. Even the 125s were oil-tight, well equipped, neatly finished and fitted with reliable electrics, which was more than could be said of much of their opposition. Helped by Honda's increasing success in Grands Prix, the roadsters started to make an impact in the showrooms.

The early Honda twin that many remember with most affection is the CB92's bigger brother, the 250cc CB72, which was first produced a year later in 1960 (but was not exported in any numbers until a couple of years later). As you might expect, the sports CB was just one development of a bulbous base-model called the C72, but this time Honda went a stage further with their modifications.

The CB72's powerplant was a wet-sump unit, and differed from the norm in running twin carburettors and a

The CB72, 250cc sports bike first produced in 1968, became an early export success.

180-degree crankshaft, the pistons rising and falling alternately. Power delivery was poor at low revs, but by 9,000rpm the CB was putting out a handy 24bhp through its four-speed gearbox.

The frame was changed from the normal pressed steel to a much stiffer tubular construction. A single large tube ran back from the steering head, then curved down to the swing-arm pivot, and was aided by a pair of smaller tubes running from steering head to cylinder head. Forks were telescopic, again an improvement over previous leading-link designs, and both brakes were powerful twin-leading-shoe drums. Flat bars, the normal humpy polished tank, a good dual seat, slick mudguards, adjustable footrests on alloy plates, and a neatly combined speedometer and rev-counter added up to a very attractive package – especially when that speedo's needle could be persuaded round to 90mph (145kph) if the tacho needle alongside was kept near its red line.

'Handling', said the American magazine *Cycle World*, 'was just about what we have come to expect of a Honda: stable and fast-cornering. Fork angle, trail, spring rates and damper settings are near-perfect, and even a fairly timid

CB72 (1960)	
Engine	Aircooled 4-valve SOHC parallel twin
Bore × stroke	54 × 54mm
Capacity	247cc
Comp. ratio	9.5:1
Claimed power	24bhp @ 9,000rpm
Carburation	2 × 22mm Biliath
Gearbox	4-speed
Tyres, front	2.75 × 18in
Rear	3.00 × 18in
Brakes, front	200mm (8in) tls drum
Rear	200mm (8in) tls drum
Wheelbase	1,295mm (51in)
Weight	153kg (337lb) dry
Fuel capacity	16.2 litres (3.6 gallons)
Top speed (approx.)	90mph (145kph)
Standing ¼-mile	17.5sec/75mph (121kph)

rider will find it very natural to ride faster and lean over farther than it is his habit to do.

'Rider position is, of necessity because of the low, flat handlebars, very "Mike Hailwood", and although it looks ferociously uncomfortable for touring, the controls and seat are positioned in such a way that it is in fact quite good.'

And the crunch came on a twisty road, where the rider of a screaming twin did not need the skill of a Hailwood – who won his first world championship on a 250cc Honda in 1961 – to give even the pilots of much bigger British machines trouble shaking him off. Many British bikers were still scornful, but with the CB72 Honda earned plenty of respect.

Parallel Motion: The CBs Whir On

Many people would argue that most of Honda's range of small-capacity twins have no place in any book that includes the word 'classic' in its title, and they have a point. After the initial impact of bikes such as the CB72 in the early and mid-1960s, few of Honda's parallel twins were particularly outstanding and few made much of a contribution to the development of the motorbike.

But, mundane as most of them were, if sales figures determine popularity then the Honda twins were some of the best-loved bikes of all. Generally competent if lacking in inspiration, they covered millions of miles all across the planet, and led countless riders towards more exciting

Early twins such as this 1963-registered 305cc C77 were heavily built, with enormous mudguards.

The CB250, the first and probably the best of its kind, as it became chubbier and less competitive over the years.

machinery. For that reason alone they are worthy of mention here.

The typical early-1970s twin was the CB250/350 design that first appeared in 1968 and lasted, with various modifications along the way, until 1976. By the standards of small-capacity twins these were physically large bikes, but they looked quite handsome (there's a vague family resemblance to the CB750) and were well equipped in typical Honda style.

The CB250 and 350 were more than just close relatives, for they were virtually the same bike. The chassis was a

tubular cradle in each case and suspension was by telescopic forks and underdamped rear shocks that made for a very interesting ride when pushed hard over bumps.

Both models (not to mention the CL trail versions, and the touring CD250) shared engine parts right down to the crankshafts, the bigger bike merely having an 8mm bigger bore which raised its capacity from 249 to 236cc. The CB250 put out 30bhp at 10,500rpm and the 350 made 36bhp at the same high engine speed, at which point they shook, rattled and rolled in true parallel-twin tradition.

'Their shortcomings included high vibration, mediocre

In 1974 Honda's four-stroke CB200 twin had two-stroke opposition from Suzuki's GT185 and Yamaha's RD200.

handling qualities when the engine was ridden hard, and some annoying engine noises. They were designed to please a large cross-section of the world's motorcyclists, and they did just that,' sneered *Cycle World* of CB350s in particular.

At least the magazine praised the CBs' 'low initial price, good fuel economy, ease of minor servicing, up-to-date styling and adequate braking qualities'. Front disc brakes were offered as an option in 1971, and three years later came an engine revision, when a sixth gear was added and numerous internal changes made.

But the CBs were growing increasingly podgy (the CB250's dry weight rose from 328lb (149kg) to 364lb (165kg) between 1968 and 1974), and meanwhile the competition was moving on. The CJ250T and CJ360T twins of 1976, with their two-into-one exhausts, plastic mudguards, lack of electric starter and return to the five-speed box, were lighter and smarter. But they were also slow, handled poorly and were generally considered a flop.

Honda replaced them only a year later, when the CB250 and 400T appeared with a complete revamp which included restyling – to a dumpy, rounded look which few people thought attractive – plus new engines featuring three valves per cylinder for better breathing, and contra-rotating balancer shafts to kill vibration.

The 400, in particular, was an impressive if less than charismatic bike. Its 44bhp engine gave 100mph (160kph)-plus performance, enough to see off Honda's own popular CB400 four, and its handling was a vast improvement over that of the old CB360s. 'The CB400T's handling, roadhold-

ing and willing engine all combine to encourage spirited riding,' said *Bike* magazine.

The CB250T, physically almost identical to the bigger model, was also a big improvement over its predecessor, although its comparatively low output of 27bhp, pushing a similar near-400lb (180kg) weight, meant that performance was nowhere near as lively. The less torquey 250 had to be rowed along on its five-speed gearbox but was capable of almost 90mph (145kph).

Much the same was true of the CB250N, which appeared

Although few would describe them as handsome, the CB250T (above) and the similar 400T of 1977 were useful all-round motorbikes.

in 1979 with much neater Eurostyling and the dubious advantage of six gears. The bike sold in its thousands, despite soggy low-rev acceleration, handling that deteriorated rapidly as the rear shocks heated up, and dubious reliability of the frequently abused engine's top-end and clutch.

The 400cc version, again, was a better bike although it shared the same marginal rear suspension. Almost as fast as much racier opposition such as Yamaha's two-stroke

---

CB400N (1979)

Engine	Aircooled 6-valve SOHC parallel twin
Bore × stroke	70.5 × 50.6mm
Capacity	395cc
Comp. ratio	9.3:1
Claimed power	43bhp @ 9,500rpm
Carburation	2 × 32mm Keihins
Gearbox	6-speed
Tyres, front	3.60 × 19in
Rear	4.10 × 18in
Brakes, front	Twin 240mm (9.4in) discs
Rear	152mm (6in) drum
Suspension, front	Telescopic forks
Rear	Twin shocks with adjustable preload
Wheelbase	1,390mm (54.7in)
Weight	176kg (387lb) wet
Fuel capacity	15 litres (3.1 gallons)
Top speed (approx.)	105mph (169kph)
Standing ¼-mile	14.5sec/90mph (145kph)

RD400, in 1979 the CB400N was good enough for *Bike* to conclude that 'as a complete motorcycle there's not much that comes near it. The futuristic styling and highly efficient engine keep it ahead of the competition and contribute to the air of quality that surrounds the machine.'

Ten years later the bike was virtually unchanged but the story was rather different. In 1986 Honda had made a fair attempt to modernize the twin with a bored-out, fancy-framed little bike called the CB350S. Three years after that they bored out the CB400 to 447cc and reintroduced it, with few other updates, as the CB450S.

The bike was manufactured in Brazil, and by 1989 standards it was a Third World motorcycle in more than its country of origin. But, if the 450S was far too slow and crude to please the purists, it was hard to question Honda's decision to continue selling the twin if they could. And it could hardly be said that they had produced no twin-cylinder alternatives in the meantime.

Growing Up: Bigger Twins, from Black Bomber to CB500T

The rumours circulated for months before the truth was at last revealed, but in spring 1965 Honda finally unveiled the bike that proved they were serious: the CB450 parallel twin (which was similar only in name to the machine that would appear twenty-four years later). Until then their biggest model had been 305cc, a mere tiddler compared to real British iron, but now the gauntlet was down.

CB450 (1965)

Engine	Aircooled 4-valve DOHC parallel twin
Bore × stroke	70 × 57.8mm
Capacity	445cc
Comp. ratio	8.5:1
Claimed power	43bhp @ 8,500rpm
Carburation	2 × 36mm Keihin
Gearbox	4-speed
Tyres, front	3.25 × 18in
Rear	3.25 × 18in
Brakes, front	200mm (8in) tls drum
Rear	180mm (7.2in) sls drum
Suspension, front	Telescopic
Rear	Twin shocks with adjustable preload
Wheelbase	1,346mm (53in)
Weight	187kg (411lb) dry
Fuel capacity	19 litres (4.2 gallons)
Top speed (approx.)	105mph (169kph)
Standing ¼-mile	15sec/85mph (137kph)

The CB450's twin-cam engine showed that Honda were no longer content to leave the big-bike market to the British.

Cycle World was in no doubt about the CB450's significance. 'Beyond any doubt, the big news item of the preceding 12 months came when Honda finally announced ("admitted" would be a better word) that there was, in fact, a new big-displacement addition to their line of motorcycles,' the magazine commented.

The 450 was not actually particularly powerful or fast. Its output of a claimed 43bhp at 8,500rpm was 4bhp down on Triumph's T120 Bonneville, for example, and the Japanese

*This high-barred version of the CB450 was sold in
America, where the bike was more successful.*

bike's claimed top speed of 112mph (180kph) proved to be
very optimistic.

But the 450's arrival was a sign that Honda were not
content to produce only small-capacity machinery, and that
they had every intention to challenge the British industry
head on. Before long, the other Japanese firms would join in
to offer big-bore alternatives to the likes of Triumph and

Norton. What had become a natural progression from small-
bore Honda to big Brit was about to end.

The CB450 was in many ways just a bigger version of the
current range of twins, though it added several new
features. The pair of cylinders was arranged vertically
above a four-speed gearbox, with heavily oversquare
dimensions of 70 × 57.8mm giving a capacity of 445cc. Like
the CB72, but unlike most other Hondas, the export bike's
crankshaft was a 180-degree unit. (Strangely, a 360-degree
version was built for the home market.)

The camchain ran up the middle of the block in the normal
way, but the big difference was that the 450 had twin cams.
An enormous endless chain drove them both via various
sprockets and guides. Valve springs were an unusual
'torsion-bar' design instead of the normal coil spring.

The frame was not the normal spine type but a tubular
cradle, which supported the hefty lump from underneath.
The rest of the chassis was very much along the lines of
smaller Hondas such as the CB72, with telescopic forks,
close-fitting front mudguard, twin-leading-shoe front drum
brake and twin rear shocks.

A humpy tank with chrome side-pieces echoed the
smaller sportsters' look too, but the CB450's black tank-
top and sidepanels soon earned it the nickname Black
Bomber. 'Meet the big black bomber – the biggest beefiest
touring twin from Japan!' ran the British importers' magazine
ads.

Touring Twin was the correct description because,
despite its lowish bars (slightly higher on the American
version), CB initials and twin cams the Bomber was softly

Man of Letters: Honda's Bike-Labelling System

Soichiro Honda could hardly have begun in a more logical way when he called his first machine the Model A, his second the Model B and his third the Model C. If only life had remained so simple.

Honda's next bike, the Model D Dream, was the first to be given a name. And, although the pattern of lettering followed fairly naturally in the immediate years to come, the sheer number of new models and variations soon created confusion.

By the early 1960s, for example, there were four different sizes of small twins alone, from 125 to 305cc, each coming in several versions: standard, sports, touring, off-road, etc. By 1967 there were *eight* different 125s, incorporating a vast permutation of engines, frames, wheels and seats.

The prefixes began by being quite straightforward. The early basic-model roadster was normally a C, with CB being the sportster (when the fours arrived, nearly all were CBs), CD the so-called tourer, CS the tourer with raised exhausts, CL the scrambler (anything with an L is off-road – with the notable exception of the GL Gold Wing), and CR the road-racer.

Less common variations included CBM high-barred sportsters, CZ monkey bikes and CYB production-based racers. Later would come the likes of the CP police bikes, the CX range of V-twins and finally the CBR fours. Other C-bikes were mopeds: CM step-thrus, CF step-thrus with small wheels, CT trail step-thrus . . .

The letter M is another common prefix, covering such varied models as the M85 Juno scooter, early ME and MF singles, and MR and MT enduro bikes. The letter X suggests off-road capabilities, while most bikes beginning with a P are mopeds. (PC covers both a moped and the enormous PC800.)

At the other end of the scale, the letters RC designate competition-based bikes, from early scramblers and factory racers to the recent RC30 sportster, whose real title is the VFR750R. The V-twins and V4s normally have a V in their prefix, logically enough, although the 1990-model ST1100 instead adopts initials previously used for a mini-bike.

Just to add to the confusion, most N-bikes are sporty two-strokes but the NTV is a plodding four-stroke. And, strangest of all, the early 125 and 250cc twins were designated '90s' and '70s' respectively. The C90 is therefore both a 1958 125cc twin and a 1990-model 89cc step-thru.

Suffixes are less widespread, and are normally used only to identify model changes, generally each year. Notable exceptions are the sporty F and touring K used to distinguish some fours, and the R which is sometimes added to suggest racetrack breeding.

Even suffixes can be misleading. The CB750 ran logically from the K0 in 1970 to the K8 in 1978. But when the CB550 arrived in 1975 it began as the K1. By then the 750 had reached K5.

When you have a range of literally dozens of bikes, most changing in some way at least every year, a little confusion is perhaps inevitable.

tuned and when tested by *Cycle World* barely managed to top the ton. It was also no lightweight, at over 400lb (180kg).

Instead, the CB450's assets turned out to be its respectable handling ('steering is light, and has a reassuringly stable feel,' said the American mag), comparative smoothness even at high revs, comfort and tractability. The novelty of twin CV carbs gave snatch-free response, and the CB was well suited to carrying a pillion.

In the end, though, the CB450 will be remembered more for what it promised or threatened than for what it delivered.

By 1974 Honda's big twin was no longer competitive, and the unreliable CB500T was a dismal flop.

That there were calls to ban the Bomber from British production racing on account of its twin cams does not disguise the fact that Honda were not to steal the British firms' performance lead until the four-cylinder CB750 appeared several years later.

American sales were quite good but in Britain the CB450 was an even slower mover in the showroom than it was on the street. Some bikes were even given clip-on bars and a splash of red paint by a dealer in a desperate attempt to make them more attractive.

The sportier factory-built follow-up predicted by some never arrived, and apart from the addition of a trail version, the CL450, in 1967 the big twin was almost ignored. In 1968 the engine was treated to the fifth gear that it should probably have had all along, and two years later the CB gained a front disc brake.

But it was becoming less competitive against the fours all the time, and the final ignominy came in 1974 when the motor was enlarged to 499cc to produce the CB500T. This was a particularly uninspiring bike, noteworthy only because of its frequent appearances in pundits' lists of all-time worst motorcycles.

Styling was instantly dated and not helped by an unattractive brown seat. Handling was distinctly marginal. Performance by mid-1970s standards was feeble, for not only did the 500T make slightly less peak power than the original Black Bomber but it lacked the traditional big-twin asset of grunt at low revs too.

'Boring' was one of the more generous adjectives used to describe the CB500T at the time – and that was before the 'world's longest camchain' began to give problems. Definitely one of Honda's classic mistakes.

Heavee Water: The Surprising CX500

It appeared in 1978, burbling and twittering (and shortly afterwards rattling) its unique greeting, grossly overweight and ugly as sin. It has been regarded with a strange mixture of respect and derision ever since. More than a decade later, though, thousands of CX500s are still resolutely clicking up the miles, and the V-twin is regarded as one of Honda's biggest successes.

The CX was an unlikely hero, with neither the looks nor the charisma to make it in any way an exciting motorcycle. It was bulky and top-heavy, and acquired the unflattering nickname of Plastic Maggot – largely due to its distinctive cylinders which stuck out – even before the addition of the fairing with which several later versions were fitted.

But it was reasonably fast, with a top speed of over 100mph (160kph) and the ability to cruise effortlessly at 80mph (130kph), and it was smooth and comfortable. Most of all it was cheap, economical, easily serviced and reliable – at least after an embarrassing early rash of crankshaft and camchain-tensioner failures had been cured.

The motor was an interesting mixture. A watercooled V-twin with cylinders splayed at 80 degrees, given a slight twist and arranged across the frame in the style long used

The CX500 in its natural habitat, covered in rust and dirt, loaded with top-box and radio, flanked by despatch riders waiting for a job in London's Carnaby Street.

by the Italian Moto Guzzi factory, it combined oversquare dimensions and four-valve cylinder heads with pushrod valve operation. A single camshaft sat high up in the crankcase, driven by a Hy-Vo chain.

Guzzi's engines had always been thought ideal for cooling by air but Honda added the bulk and weight of watercooling, which helped lift on-the-road mass above 450lb (200kg). Peak power of 50bhp came as high as 9,000rpm, but there was a decent amount of torque throughout the range.

CX500 (1978)

Engine	Watercooled 80-degree pushrod transverse V-twin
Bore × stroke	78 × 52mm
Capacity	496cc
Comp. ratio	10:1
Claimed power	50bhp @ 9,000rpm
Carburation	2 × 35mm Keihin
Gearbox	5-speed
Tyres, front	3.25 × 19in
Rear	3.75 × 18in
Brakes, front	Twin 240mm (9.4in) discs
Rear	190mm (7.5in) sls drum
Suspension, front	Telescopic
Rear	Twin shocks with adjustable preload
Wheelbase	1,455mm (57.3in)
Weight	212kg (467lb) wet
Fuel capacity	17 litres (3.7 gallons)
Top speed (approx.)	105mph (169kph)
Standing ¼-mile	14.5sec/90mph (145kph)

The CX's watercooling and shaft-drive marked it as a long-distance bike from the word go – at one stage Honda themselves described the early model as a GL500, or mini-Gold Wing – and its chassis was designed in the same style around a hefty spine frame.

Suspension was soft and sometimes shown up by all that weight, but within reason the CX handled pretty well. Its brakes were good, and the Honda's sensible riding position,

reasonable fuel range and enormously thick seat all helped make it an ideal long-haul companion.

Its nasty styling, not helped by a strange headlamp nacelle and the bulk of the radiator, combined with its excessive weight to ensure that the CX never found favour with fast-touring riders in the way that Honda had doubtless hoped. *SuperBike* magazine spoke for many when they said 'the CX is smooth, urbane, civilised, debonair, quiet-spoken and good mannered. If you like that sort of thing, fine. I'd rush out and buy a Kawasaki Z650.'

But, if anyone was in any doubt about the CX500's suitability for covering long distances with a minimum of fuss, then the bike's swift acceptance by the motorcycle couriers who ride all day for a living spoke volumes. Despatch riders took to it in huge numbers. London, in particular, was soon teeming with CXs notable for their crackling radios, lashed-on luggage systems and patched-up cosmetics.

The CX500 proved itself to be the classic camel of motorcycling that would plod faithfully onwards for ever and a day. In that respect, certainly nothing before or since has matched it.

Veering Towards Absurdity: The CX500 Turbo

If there is one word that best describes the original CX500, it is perhaps 'sensible' or 'practical'. The high-handlebarred CX500C custom version that followed a couple of years

CX500 Turbo (1981)

Engine	Watercooled 80-degree pushrod transverse V-twin, turbocharged
Bore × stroke	78 × 52mm
Capacity	497cc
Comp. ratio	7.2:1
Claimed power	82bhp @ 8,000rpm
Carburation	Computerized fuel injection
Gearbox	5-speed
Tyres, front	3.50 × 18in
Rear	120/70 × 17in
Brakes, front	Twin 280mm (11in) discs
Rear	280mm (11in) disc
Suspension, front	Telescopic with air assistance and TRAC anti-dive
Rear	Pro-Link monoshock with air assistance
Wheelbase	1,495mm (58.9in)
Weight	240kg (527lb)
Fuel capacity	20 litres (4.3 gallons)
Top speed (approx.)	125mph (200kph)
Standing ¼-mile	12.5sec/100mph (160kph)

later was less so, and the CX that Honda launched in late 1981 was about as far removed from a sensible motorcycle as it was possible to get.

In fact the Turbo was not so much a motorbike as a corporate statement: behold and admire, all ye doubters, for this is what Honda's engineers can do. At the time, turbocharging was an increasingly popular way of gaining

big horsepower increases, by fitting an aftermarket unit to a 1,000cc Kawasaki or some other large-capacity multi whose relatively small, regular power impulses are most suited to its application. (Even then, most people thought it not worth the bother.)

Honda chose instead to flaunt their prowess by turbocharging a middleweight V-twin, which made life almost as difficult as possible. That the result turned out to be even a half-way decent motorbike was therefore quite commend-

The tiny turbocharger below the headstock of the CX500 Turbo hints at its frightening complexity.

able, and within the limitations of its vast weight, size, complexity and expense the CX500 Turbo was a qualified success. Unfortunately, those limitations could not be overcome even by Honda.

The turbocharger itself was the world's smallest, its rotors less than 2in in diameter, and it spun at a frightening 200,000rpm to give maximum boost of 18.5psi and lift the CX's horsepower peak from 50 to 82bhp at 8,000rpm. The stock crankcases were deemed strong enough to cope but naturally much of the engine was up-rated. A heftier crankshaft and clutch, beefier conrods and Honda's first production-spec forged pistons all helped keep it together.

The bike itself, on the other hand, was one of the world's largest. The CX chassis was redesigned to incorporate Honda's Pro-Link monoshock rear end. Forks, wheels and brakes were all increased in size, and the bike gained a large and very efficient pearl-white fairing which did much to emphasize the CX's new *gran turismo* image. Especially when it came with the word 'Turbo' (or 'Obrut', for the benefit of British rear-view mirrors) emblazoned in red capitals across its front.

The bike's main problem was that its performance did not live up to expectations. Given its 527lb (239kg) of dry weight, the CX was not a bad handler. If its sheer bulk and mass were rarely far from the rider's mind, then at least the suspension was fairly good and the Turbo was reassuringly stable even at speed. Only in slow corners was it a real handful.

A more serious problem was lack of sheer speed, for despite all its complexity the Turbo was good for only about 125mph (200kph), and its acceleration was disappointing. And then there was the predictable turbo lag, the delay between throttle opening and engine response that almost all turbocharged vehicles are stuck with to a degree.

'Potter along gently at low rpm and a crack of throttle, and the delay before the generation of full boost will occupy whole seconds,' said *Bike*. 'When you snap open the throttle you do not feel a kick in the posterior, but a surge of progressively developing acceleration . . . If you want to grab a whole handful and explode out of some hostile hole, you cannot.'

American *Cycle* was even more critical: 'Boost [at slow speeds] was just too difficult to control; the power surge in low gears caused the rear tire to slither on the sandblown road . . . As the hours rolled by, it became more and more apparent that the Turbo was built for first impressions. It seemed like a tart, and underneath the make-up lurked a bike so divergent that its function was secondary to the celebration of complexity.

'The CX500 Turbo is a collection of mosts, not bests. It is flashy, complex and expensive, but underneath, many of its pieces are quite modest. As a showcase the Turbo is a success, but it serves Honda better than it serves its owner.'

It would take another couple of years, and the arrival of the 650cc Turbo, before the machine came close to matching the image. The bigger bike had less lag, more torque and more horsepower – a maximum of 100bhp at 8,000rpm. It was still a large, complicated animal but when you opened

The bigger CX650 Turbo turned out to be very useful for posing, if not for riding, as rising star Wayne Gardner soon found out.

the throttle it now took off at a thrillingly rapid rate, and thundered up to almost 135mph (217kph).

But, for all its complexity and excitement, the Turbo was still barely quicker than much simpler alternatives such as Honda's own CB900 four, a fact that was lost neither on the public nor – eventually – on the manufacturers. When each of the major Japanese firms had produced a turbo-bike, they quietly abandoned the idea. The new breed that had been heralded by Honda's great white elephant was extinct.

Turn of the Worm:
The VT500 and Derivatives

At the same time that the bigger Turbo was launched, Honda also uprated the standard CX to a similar capacity to produce the CX650E. A year earlier, in 1982, the 500 had received a Pro-Link rear end and Eurostyle lines reminiscent of many other Hondas of the early 1980s; now the V-twin gained extra bottom-end torque and an extra peak 14bhp, giving a total of 64bhp at 8,000rpm.

The result was a pretty competent motorbike. The CX650E still had the old top-heaviness problem, and it was prone to occasional wallowing in fast bends, but it would now rumble up to over 110mph (177kph) and deliver comfortable high-speed cruising all day long. (The fully faired GL650 Silver Wing, which arrived a year later, offered more of the same at the expense of enormous width and yet more weight – a real mini-Gold Wing at last.)

But Honda's most important new V-twin in 1983 was the one that turned the engine round in the frame: the VT500. In fact the VT motor was nothing like the old CX lump. The angle of its V was smaller, 52 degrees against 80; and single overhead cams opened three valves per cylinder (each with two spark plugs), instead of pushrods opening four.

There were many similarities between the two, though, notably the use of watercooling and shaft drive, and the claimed maximum output of 50bhp that the new 500 shared with the original CX. Styling was much more on the lines of the later transverse twins, with neat integrated tank and sidepanels, plus a uselessly small handlebar fairing.

The VT was similarly comfortable and well equipped but it was almost as uninspiring to ride as the CX and it had some silly faults. Fitting a more protective fairing or hard luggage was difficult, access to the engine for valve adjustment was complicated, and the British-spec enclosed front disc brake was both inaccessible and prone to fade under hard use.

But the VT offered some distinct advantages too. It was much narrower, slightly lighter overall, less top-heavy and generally better-looking than the CXs. It handled fairly well, and proved to be commendably reliable from the

The VT500 of 1983 had a watercooled V-twin engine whose cylinders sat longitudinally in the frame.

outset. Only the clutch gave more than occasional problems, sometimes suffering under the heavy left hand of the many despatch riders who adopted the bike as the CX500 of the late 1980s.

The in-line V-twin engine, too, would find itself popping up in a variety of new guises over the years. (An in-line V engine is one in which the crankshaft runs at right angles to the body line of the bike, as opposed to a transverse V, in which the crankshaft runs along the body line.) In 1987 it was enlarged to 583cc, put in a semi-trail bike chassis featuring a big 21in front wheel, hidden beneath a swoopily integrated fairing-tank unit (based very loosely on Paris–Dakar Rally styling) and called the Transalp.

The combination sounds a strange one but the result was a surprisingly pleasant bike. At almost 400lb (180kg) dry, the Transalp was always going to be a handful off road, but the tall bike's agility, excellent suspension and tractable motor proved well up to the odd excursion into the rough. On the road it was even better. Although the handlebars were wide and fairly high, the fairing's screen gave enough protection to make 80mph (130kph)-plus cruising possible as long as the rider didn't mind some vibration coming through from the engine.

The bike would carry a pillion more happily than many race-replica roadsters, and although it sold slowly in Britain it was popular on the Continent. Honda even organized an annual Transalp Rally in its honour, leading groups of similarly mounted enthusiasts on lengthy crash-and-burn trips through Scandinavia or Spain. Excellent fun, especially if you were a spares dealer.

From the Transalp's 650cc motor Honda developed in two directions. One was further off-road, where the XRV650 Africa Twin adopted full-blown Paris–Dakar styling, complete with twin-headlamp fairing, an enormous petrol tank seemingly capable of crossing the Sahara in one hit, twin front disc brakes and much unwanted extra weight and height.

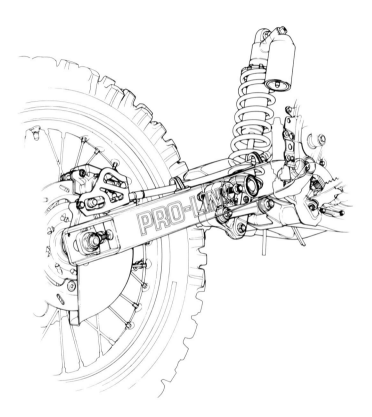

Honda's patented monoshock Pro-Link suspension system, first used on motocross bikes to give a rising-rate action, was adapted for use on roadsters such as the CX Turbo in the early 1980s.

600V Transalp (1987)

Engine	Watercooled 6-valve SOHC 52-degree in-line V-twin
Bore × stroke	75 × 66mm
Capacity	583cc
Comp. ratio	9.2:1
Claimed power	55bhp @ 8,000rpm
Carburation	2 × 32mm Keihin
Gearbox	5-speed
Tyres, front	90/90 × 21in
Rear	130/80 × 17in
Brakes, front	276mm (10.9in) discs
Rear	130mm (5.1in) sls drum
Suspension, front	Telescopic with air assistance
Rear	Pro-Link monoshock with adjustable preload
Wheelbase	1,505mm (59.2in)
Weight	175kg (385lb)
Fuel capacity	18 litres (4 gallons)
Top speed (approx.)	105mph (185kph)
Standing ¼-mile	14sec/95mph (153kph)

The XRV650, although too big to be manageable by most riders on the dirt, made a surprisingly good roadster if your inside-leg measurement was sufficient to keep it upright at the traffic lights. Bright colours, apparent competitive intent and long-travel suspension made it ideal for comfortable posing. But, when the motor was then bored and stroked to 742cc to power the Africa Twin 750, the joke had gone just too far.

The bigger motor was only marginally more responsive at low speeds but noticeably harsher at higher revs. And the bike itself, now scaling more than 500lb (227kg) with a full petrol tank, was too heavy, too tall and too expensive to be of interest to all but the very serious or the very vain.

The other direction Honda went in was almost the complete opposite, for while the Africa Twin was ultimately a rather silly motorcycle the NTV600's problem was that it was just too sensible to be much fun.

The faithful 583cc V-twin motor was retained, and bolted into a sturdy-looking perimeter frame which was backed up by broad 17in wheels (the sporting trend in 1988) and Honda's stylish single-sided swing arm. But if the cycle parts' specification promised spirited handling, the NTV600 was let down by mediocre suspension and rather too much weight.

The engine's limited power output and flat delivery inspired little excitement either – all of which would not have mattered too much if the shaft-driven Revere, as it was named (fortunate Americans were treated to a sportier chain-drive version instead), had provided the reliable budget motorcycling of its CX and VT forebears. Unfortunately,

though, it was priced at the level of much more interesting machinery, and had little chance of success.

Honda's most interesting twin of the late 1980s was paradoxically also the most sanitized, even more so than the NTV. The PC800 Pacific Coast was the company's attempt to reverse a drastic situation in America, where in 1989 overall two-wheeled sales were down by a third over the previous year, a rejuvenated Harley-Davidson had captured

PC800 Pacific Coast (1989)	
Engine	Watercooled 6-valve SOHC 45-degree in-line V-twin
Bore × stroke	79.5 × 80.6mm
Capacity	800cc
Comp. ratio	9:1
Claimed power	50bhp @ 7,000rpm
Carburation	2 × 36mm Keihin
Gearbox	5-speed
Tyres, front	120/80 × 17in
Rear	140/80 × 15in
Brakes, front	Twin 276mm (10.9in) discs
Rear	Sls drum
Suspension, front	Telescopic
Rear	Twin shocks with adjustable preload
Wheelbase	1,555mm (61.2in)
Weight	262kg (578lb) dry
Fuel capacity	16 litres (3.5 gallons)
Top speed (approx.)	115mph (185kph)
Standing ¼-mile	14sec/90mph (145kph)

more than half the big-bike buyers, and once-mighty Honda's share of the marketing sector had been eroded to a worrying degree.

The Pacific Coast was conceived to expand the motorcycle market by capturing people who did not already ride a bike at all. 'We reinvented the motorcycle market once before, in the early sixties,' said American Honda's marketing chief at the bike's introduction. 'And we can do it again.'

Designed by Honda's car division to present the most accessible, least aggressive face of two-wheeled travel, the PC hid its engine deep beneath vast acres of grey-and-cream plastic. Smooth styling hid anything that might have put off the non-motorcyclists by looking frighteningly mechanical, and a huge car-type trunk, big enough for two crash-helmets and more, swung up at the pull of a lever. Tucked away out of sight and quietened by rubber shrouds as well as by the bodywork, the 800cc V-twin – almost identical to that in the US-spec VT800 Shadow custom bike – used rubber-mounting, hydraulically adjusted valves and the traditional VT family shaft drive to make it as smooth and maintenance-free as possible.

The 50bhp engine put out plenty of grunt in the mid-range and was powerful enough to send even the broad Coast up to a top speed approaching 120mph (193kph). Given the PC's marshmallow-like looks, its handling might have been expected to be equally soft. But beneath all its bodywork the Coast was lighter than it looked, at 578lb (264kg) dry, and its non-adjustable anti-dive-equipped forks, twin shocks, double front discs and rear drum brake gave an adequate mix of comfort, cornering and stopping power.

Despite spending a small fortune on advertising, American Honda failed to tempt non-motorcyclists to buy the PC800 Pacific Coast.

For a bike that promised to be boring, the Coast was actually surprisingly good fun, and it received favourable reviews on both sides of the Atlantic. (Like the 650 Africa Twin, the PC was not officially offered in Britain but was imported by specialist dealers.)

But, unfortunately for Honda, being better to ride than to look at did not guarantee that its target audience of affluent Americans would spend dollars (at almost $8,000, it wasn't cheap) on the bike instead of on golf or some other leisure pursuit. Despite heavy advertising on television and in general-interest magazines, the Pacific Coast sold slowly, and Honda's slump continued into the 1990s.

3

Playing Straight
The In-Line Multis

CB750: Four Is More

In these days of 170mph (275kph) superbikes, when middle-weights which barely rate a second glance can top 140mph (225 kph) and when competition among manufacturers is so fierce that a new model rarely stands head and shoulders out of the crowd, it is hard to appreciate just how much impact Honda's four- cylinder CB750 made when it was first seen at the 1968 Tokyo Show.

The 750's line-up of cylinders and exhaust pipes was sensational enough on its own. Until the Honda's arrival, mass-produced fours simply did not exist. Excluding the odd hand-built MV Agusta, large-capacity motorcycles were limited to triples from Kawasaki and Triumph, or twins from Suzuki and BMW.

Not only did the CB750 end all that, but it did so at a competitive price and with an unbeatable level of sophistication. Rivals such as Kawasaki's 500cc Mach III and Triumph's 750 Trident might have come close to the

Honda's top speed of a shade over 120mph (193kph), but neither of these three-cylinder bikes could approach the CB's smoothness or its lavish specification, which added a front disc brake and electric starter to Honda's reputation for reliability and good electrics.

The performance came from an aircooled engine which, while it undoubtedly put to good use much knowledge gained over the years from Honda's many racing multis, differed from the predominantly sixteen valve DOHC racers in using a single overhead camshaft (driven by chain up the centre of the engine) and two valves per cylinder. Its output of 67bhp at a restrained 8,000rpm was quite enough to get the adrenalin flowing – and the order-books bulging – at the time.

The angular motor's barrels leant forward slightly in a duplex steel frame; from this frame were hung gaitered forks and conventional twin shocks with a choice of three preload positions. Designed as an all-rounder with one eye on the lucrative, money-making American market, the

Honda was a physically big bike with a broad seat and high, wide handlebars.

The motorcycling public were stunned, and so were Honda's rival manufacturers. When the CB750 was revealed, Kawasaki were rumoured to have abandoned advanced plans for a 750cc four-stroke four of their own. They were impressed enough not to return with the Z900 for another four years.

The testers of the day went into overdrive, coining the word 'superbike' in the CB750's honour (though Triumph, who narrowly beat Honda into production with their Trident, might disagree). The British bike paper *Motor Cycle* reported that 'docile and tractable, the engine purrs happily at 3,000rpm in top. Tweak the grip and the pick-up is unhesitant; it is so deceptively smooth that you are forgiven for thinking it almost sluggish until the speedometer and wind pressure tell the truth.

CB750 (1969)	
Engine	Aircooled 8-valve SOHC transverse four
Bore × stroke	61 × 63mm
Capacity	736cc
Comp. ratio	9:1
Claimed power	67bhp @ 8,000rpm
Carburation	4 × 28mm Keihin
Gearbox	5-speed
Tyres, front	3.25 × 19in
Rear	4.00 × 18in
Brakes, front	290mm (11.5in) disc
Rear	180mm (7.1in) sls drum
Suspension, front	Telescopic
Rear	Twin shock absorbers
Wheelbase	1448mm (57in)
Weight	239kg (526lb) wet
Fuel capacity	17 litres (3.8 gallons)
Top speed (approx.)	123mph (198kph)
Standing ¼-mile	13.5sec/100mph (160kph)

The CB750 caused a sensation at the Tokyo Show in October 1968.

*Undisputed King of the Road in 1969, the
CB750 combined 120mph (193kph) performance
with firm suspension and a front disc brake.*

'A combination of complete smoothness and effortless torque waft you up to the 90s so rapidly that only the alarming speed at which you rush up to the corners dispels the illusion.'

The big, heavy 750 would later come under fire for frame flex and marginal suspension, but few limitations were reported after a test on Germany's uniquely demanding Nurburgring racetrack. 'For a machine of its bulk the Honda handled well. Occasionally I entered corners quicker than I should have done and had to keep the brakes on. Extra effort was then required to lay the model over and this caused some tail-wagging.

'But normally cornering was extremely steady, with the model leeching to whatever line I chose. Front and rear suspension are well-matched, with rebound damping firm enough to prevent the wallowing and bouncing so often associated with Japanese bikes.

'The single disc brake was smoother than is usual with a twin-leading-shoe drum, and the sensitivity of the hydraulic action was reassuring on the dodgy surfaces. Under fierce braking both tyres gripped extremely well – far better than any previous Japanese covers with which I have had experience.'

When the 750 was released in 1969 the American market was dominant, and much of the bike's early production went to the States. *Cycle World* was impressed, though it rated the suspension 'comfortable but decidedly firm' and found that 'the bike may begin a light up-and-down oscillation over regular tar joints' due to the forks' resistance to initial movement.

The introduction to their test perhaps summed up the CB750's appeal most graphically: 'Tired of people not noticing? In past years, motorcycling marked you as a man apart. But now everyone rides a motorcycle, and things don't seem the same any more.

'The only thing that could relight your fire is the very best road bike in the world. Owning a bike like this, you could thumb your nose at the Honda Motor Company, which is most responsible for seeing that hordes of *nouveau* riders crowd you on your private road.

'But if you had the finest of all production machines, this two-wheeled answer to Ferrari-Porsche-Lamborghini, you would be riding a Honda 750cc four-cylinder. Soichiro-San would have the last laugh.'

Shaping the Superbike: From K1 to F2

Soichiro was indeed entitled to laugh, for the four was hugely successful all over the world and would continue to sell steadily for many years. It was the bike of the 1970s, setting the standards that other manufacturers had to match, and its impressively reliable single-cam engine formed the heart of thousands of race bikes and custom bikes all over the world.

The CB750 was also modified in a variety of ways by Honda themselves over the years, although after that huge initial splash the bike was allowed to remain in much the same form right up until 1976 – gradually losing ground to the opposition all the time.

Early changes were minor. In 1970 the K0 version gained a slightly lighter throttle, thanks to a revised carburettor-opening system: a pair of cables and a rod replaced the original four-cable set-up. The next year saw the K1 version, with uprated suspension and cosmetic changes to the petrol tank, seat, side panel and oil tank. (Unusually for Honda, the 750 motor had a dry sump, with the oil tank

The CB750's single-cam engine proved to be impressively reliable.

below the seat on the right.) A year later it gained a new set of warning lights on the dashboard, and became the K2.

By 1973 Kawasaki's twin-cam 900cc Z1 had appeared to steal much of the CB750's four-pot thunder. The Honda, meanwhile, had begun to fall victim to the steady detuning process deemed necessary to reduce emissions and satisfy American environmentalists. The K3 still managed a healthy enough 121mph (194kph) when tested by *Bike*

An original CB750 from 1968 alongside a later K4 version (right) at the Honda Owners' Club stand of the BMF (British Motorcyclists Federation) Rally in 1990.

magazine – but the Z1 tested alongside put that figure into perspective with its 133mph (214kph) top speed. Standing quarter-mile times were 13.67sec and 12.46sec respectively, giving a clear performance edge to the Kawasaki.

The bigger bike handled better, too, but it vibrated more and cost £1,088 to the Honda's £849. The CB750 was rated 'hard to beat as an all-round machine if you want power allied to reliability', and was reckoned to be the bike to satisfy riders 'who don't want, or can't afford to push things

a stage further'. The Honda's reign as king was over, although it could still show a clean quartet of silencers to most things on the road.

The first real update did not come until 1976, when the CB750F was launched in an attempt to add a bit of zip to the flagging four. This had narrow, flattish handlebars, footrests set back a couple of inches, restyled bodywork with a squarer tank and a trendy plastic tail-section, and a four-into-one exhaust system instead of the now dated four-into-four. The pipe wasn't loud but the vivid yellow colour scheme made up for it.

Unfortunately, the engine was virtually unchanged and, although still rated at 67bhp, seemed to have lost even more of its stuffing to the noise lobby. Top speed was down to around 115mph (185kph), which made Honda's 'Super Sports' label look a bit sick.

The 750F's wet-weather performance was typically awful for a Japanese bike of the time, too, with brakes (now discs at both ends) and tyres which caused many a heart-stopping moment in the rain. But its handling was much improved: lighter steering and increased stability coming from a modified frame, new suspension, reduced fork angle and a slight increase in wheelbase.

Bike's tester was impressed: 'The comfort of the riding position at sustained high speeds, the smoothness of the motor and transmission right through the rev range, and the effortless way it can confidently be flicked through the tightest and bumpiest bends, brings me to the conclusion that the 750F is my idea of what a fast tourer ought to be.'

Meanwhile, the four-pipe 750 was still around and had

become a real tourer, its larger fuel tank giving increased range at the expense of distinctly dumpy looks. By 1977 Honda had reached the K7 model, and that bike's smoothness was still an asset for gentle use. But its suspension gave a hairy ride if pushed hard on bumpy roads. Compared with the likes of Suzuki's twin-cam GS750 and even Kawasaki's popular Z650, the venerable CB showed its age.

Honda had one last trick up their sleeve for the CB750. That year they brought out the F2, a hotted-up version of the F1 which at last combined a modern chassis with the original 750's power and a bit more besides.

The long-suffering 736cc motor was painted black and treated to bigger valves, a new cam and redesigned pistons. The pipe was new and better tucked in, while carbs with accelerator pumps helped to push output to a claimed 73bhp at 9,000rpm. Although the F2 was a little peakier than

CB750F2 (1977)

Engine	Aircooled 8-valve SOHC transverse four
Bore × stroke	61 × 63mm
Capacity	736cc
Comp. ratio	9:1
Claimed power	73bhp @ 9,000rpm
Carburation	4 × 28mm Keihin
Gearbox	5-speed
Tyres, front	3.25 × 19in
Rear	4.00 × 18in
Brakes, front	Twin 276mm (10.9in) discs
Rear	296mm (11.6in) disc
Suspension, front	Telescopic
Rear	Twin shock absorbers
Wheelbase	1,494mm (58.8in)
Weight	241kg (530lb) wet
Fuel capacity	17 litres (3.7 gallons)
Top speed (approx.)	125mph (200kph)
Standing ¼-mile	13.5sec/105mph (169kph)

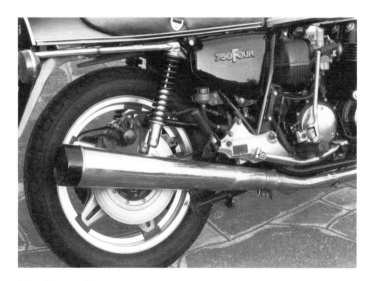

The CB750 F2 had a four-into-one exhaust and Comstar wheels, making it the best yet, but by 1977 the single-cam engine's days were numbered.

previous models, at least it was now capable of around 125mph (200kph). It also stopped better than anything that had gone before, thanks to the twin front discs it should have had years earlier. And it wore an early form of the composite Comstar wheels which Honda were to use for many years, with steel spokes bolted to an alloy hub and riveted to an alloy rim.

The CB750F2 made nothing like the impact of that first bike back in 1969, of course. But in absolute terms it was the best of Honda's single-cam 750s. And it wasn't a bad way to end the line.

Double Trouble:
The Twin-Cam 750 Fours

Having finally come up with a competent chassis for the F2's faithful old engine, Honda were expected to produce great things when the much-rumoured DOHC 750 was introduced in 1979. In fact the CB750K turned out to be very much a development of the K-series models, as its name suggests, with portly looks and four pipes.

Its engine certainly promised to be the answer – lots of bright alloy; sixteen valves opened via buckets-and-shims, the twin cams driven by a Hy-Vo chain up the centre of the barrels; a healthy 77bhp at 9,000rpm, giving it a 9bhp advantage over Suzuki's GS750.

So it proved on the road, where testers raved about the stream of smooth, steady power from low revs. The bike was comfortable, too, with a big seat and rider-friendly

ergonomics. But that was where the compliments ended. Braking from the twin front discs' single-piston calipers was rated only adequate, and the K's handling was far worse than that.

Suspension at both ends was horribly soft, and *Bike*'s tester was driven to snarl: 'For gentle touring the big Honda has few rivals but when pushed hard it can be a real dog, and at times feels downright dangerous. The magnificent engine is wasted in a mediocre chassis whose high-speed cornering ability is severely hampered by under-sprung shocks, too-soft springs and unbalanced braking.'

Unfortunately for Honda, even that was only half the problem. The K model's saving grace, its sweet engine, then turned nasty. First it developed the knack of blowing a gearbox sprocket oil seal, which could result in oil all over the rear tyre. Then the Hy-Vo camchain joined in, giving a death-rattle before either snapping or working itself through the front of the barrel.

All in all, the CB750K was a woefully disappointing bike. Its 1981 replacement, the 750F, could only be better, and it was – though the camchain problems were still not totally cured, and even the F model's handling was not always perfect.

The styling, at least, was universally praised. Slimmer and with its petrol tank neatly blended into the sidepanels, the bike looked much sportier, and followed the 'Eurostyle' lines of the DOHC CB900 Bol d'Or which had been released in Europe the year before. (Ironically, the 750F was available in America a year before it came to Europe.)

A four-into-two exhaust system pushed power up to

79bhp, and there were numerous changes to the chassis. The frame's downtubes and the swing arm were thickened, and the K's soggy shocks were replaced by multi-adjustable FVQ units which, despite picking up the nickname 'Fade Very Quicklies', were a big improvement.

Brakes were also uprated, and worked well except in the rain. Although the 750F wriggled about rather worryingly on white lines, and was no faster than the original CB750 of more than ten years earlier, it was generally reckoned to be the best 750cc Honda so far. 'Comfortable to ride, easy to steer and with engine characteristics so smooth that the FA encourages you to keep riding it all day,' concluded the now deceased British magazine *The Biker*.

CBX750: Retiring with Dignity

It was ironic that by the time Honda really got their in-line 750 sorted out, with the 1984 launch of the CBX, the world had moved on and left the bike behind. It was doubly ironic that Honda themselves, with their V4s, were the company which did most to make the CBX750 forgettable.

Taken by itself, the CBX was a very useful all-round motorbike. Its engine was yet another development of the twin-cam motor, its much more oversquare dimensions of 67 × 53mm producing a best-yet output of 91bhp. Another change was the adoption of hydraulic tappets, which made valve adjustment a chore of the past. More importantly, time would reveal the motor to be much more reliable than some of its predecessors.

CB750FA (1981)	
Engine	Aircooled 16-valve DOHC transverse four
Bore × stroke	62 × 62mm
Capacity	748cc
Comp. ratio	9:1
Claimed power	79bhp @ 9,000rpm
Carburation	4 × 30mm Keihin
Gearbox	5-speed
Tyres, front	3.25 × 19in
Rear	4.00 × 18in
Brakes, front	Twin 280mm (11in) discs
Rear	292mm (11.5in) disc
Suspension, front	Telescopic
Rear	Twin shocks, adjustable for preload, compression and rebound damping
Wheelbase	1,520mm (59.8in)
Weight	240kg (530lb) wet
Fuel capacity	20 litres (4.4 gallons)
Top speed (approx.)	125mph (200kph)
Standing ¼-mile	12.8sec/105mph (169kph)

The rest of the bike bore little resemblance to previous models. Incorporated into its neat, angular styling were such mid-1980s style accessories as a half-fairing, bellypan, 16in front wheel, TRAC anti-dive and Pro-Link single-shock suspension.

Most of it worked, for the CBX raced up to about 125mph (200kph), coped with sustained high speed effort-

CBX750 (1984)

Engine	Aircooled 16-valve DOHC transverse four
Bore × stroke	67 × 53mm
Capacity	747cc
Comp. ratio	9.3:1
Claimed power	91bhp @ 8,500rpm
Carburation	4 × 34mm CV
Gearbox	6-speed
Tyres, front	100/90 × 16in
Rear	130/80 × 18in
Brakes, front	Twin 250mm (10in) discs
Rear	250mm (10in) disc
Suspension, front	Telescopic, air-assisted, with TRAC anti-dive
Rear	Pro-Link monoshock, air-assisted, with adjustable rebound damping
Wheelbase	1,466mm (57.7in)
Weight	222kg (490lb)
Fuel capacity	22 litres (4.8 gallons)
Top speed (approx.)	125mph (200kph)
Standing ¼-mile	12.6sec/108mph (174kph)

lessly, and handled very well indeed. Steering was light and precise, suspension excellent and there were few bikes faster than a CBX750 if its rider was in the mood.

Unfortunately, the bike had to be ridden aggressively if you were going to get the best from it. Finding the final couple of horsepower had apparently removed most of the mid-range muscle for which Honda's 750s had become known over the years. Nothing much happened below 7,500rpm, which explained the adoption of a six-speed gearbox.

When compared with the opposition – both Kawasaki's and Suzuki's 750cc fours were cheaper and more powerful – or Honda's own range of V4s, which by 1984 included 500 and 1,000cc bikes as well as the VF750, the poor CBX didn't quite match up. Honda's aircooled 750cc four died in obscurity, having realized its potential a couple of years too late.

Small Fours: The CB500 and Derivatives

Back in the early 1970s it had not taken Honda long to come up with an encore to the all-conquering CB750. A smaller model, the CB500 four, arrived in 1971 and, although by no means as important, was in many respects an even better machine.

The CB500 had all the features that had made its bigger brother the boss of the street: electric start, indicators, disc brake – and, of course, those four seductive cylinders. It even added the novelty of a helmet lock (these things mattered in 1971). And, while the 750 was a physically large lump of motorcycle which needed a certain amount of muscle to be used to the full, the 500 provided much the same thrills in a less overbearing package.

At 427lb (194kg) ready-to-roll it was about 80lb (36kg) lighter than the 750, and it was also lower, shorter, quieter and a little more refined. Putting out a claimed maximum of 50bhp at 9,000rpm, the CB500 had a slightly better power-to-weight ratio than the big bike and was almost a match for it on the road.

The new motor was an oversquare version of the single-cam 750cc lump, with a few differences in its layout. Instead of running in plain bearings, the single camshaft turned directly in the cylinder head. Lubrication was therefore even more important, and was changed to the wet-sump

Smaller and lighter than its 750cc forebear, the 1971 CB500 was more manageable and almost as quick.

CB500 (1971)

Engine	Aircooled 8-valve SOHC transverse four
Bore × stroke	56 × 50.6mm
Capacity	498cc
Comp. ratio	9:1
Claimed power	50bhp @ 9,000rpm
Carburation	4 × 22mm Keihin
Gearbox	5-speed
Tyres, front	3.25 × 19in
Rear	3.50 × 18in
Brakes, front	Twin 260mm (10.3in) discs
Rear	180mm (7in) drum
Suspension, front	Telescopic
Rear	Twin shocks with adjustable preload
Wheelbase	1,397mm (55in)
Weight	194kg (427lb) wet
Fuel capacity	14 litres (3.1 gallons)
Top speed (approx.)	102mph (164kph)
Standing ¼-mile	14.7sec/88mph (142kph)

system – keeping oil in the crankcases instead of using a separate 750-style tank – that has been favoured by Honda ever since.

The motor also differed from the 750 engine in using an 'inverted-tooth' Hy-Vo primary chain instead of a pair of conventional chains. The transmission was sometimes let down by a slipping clutch or sticking gearbox, but for the most part the engine was as reliable as it was smooth. (The

Like the CB750, the later CB550 came in sports and touring models. This is the K3 tourer of 1977.

500's main failings would prove to be its rear drum brake, which was prone to cracking, and its distinctive silencers, which would quickly rot.)

On the road the gutsy little powerplant made the bike respectably quick and commendably economical. The 500 would just about top the ton under good conditions, and gave around 50mpg even when ridden hard.

Best of all, its handling meant that the performance was very usable. The frame was a double-cradle affair looking like a scaled-down 750 trellis. Forks were well behaved, and only a pair of rather soft and underdamped rear shocks let down the ride.

'The Honda could be effortlessly laid into corners with gusto and a handful of horses, and it wouldn't baulk from a chosen line even on the tightest of chicanes,' raved *Bike*. 'Keel it over and keep the power on – the Honda can handle it. Most impressive, and a bundle of fun for scratchers.'

Cycle World was just as enthusiastic: 'Virtually vibration-free performance, high cruising speed, spirited acceleration, good handling qualities, excellent fuel economy . . . All told, the Honda CB500 is perhaps the finest combination of superb engineering and deluxe features we've ever come across.'

Praise cannot be much more generous than that, even allowing for new-model hype, and not surprisingly the CB500 was a success. It continued with little change until 1975, when its motor was bored out to 544cc to produce two CB550 models, the single-piped F1 and the tubbier four-piped K1.

Café Society: Honda Specials in the Seventies

Honda might not have been keen to modify their CB750 much in the early 1970s, but demand from riders wanting extra performance resulted in a host of specials with fairings, fancy frames and/or hotted-up engines.

Dave Degens, the former racer who made his name by combining Triumph engines and Norton chassis to make Tritons in the 1960s, was one of the first. In 1972 his Dresda firm came up with a tubular-framed double-disc-braked 'café racer' which shed 100lb (45kg) of the standard Honda's weight. With its standard engine helped by a loud four-into-one exhaust, the Dresda's sleek half-fairing and low clip-on handlebars helped raise top speed towards 130mph (210kph).

By 1974 there were several more variations on the theme. Rickman, another well-known engineering firm, produced their own chassis using similar Reynolds tubing. The Rickman had only a single front disc but its bodywork was neater than the Dresda's; like that bike, it added almost half as much again to the price of the 750.

Other firms attacked the Honda's engine as well as its chassis. Read–Titon bored the engine to 810cc, a popular capacity for big-bore Hondas of the day, and bolted a fairing, tank, seat unit and new shocks to the standard frame.

Another former racer, Paul Dunstall, went furthest, boring the motor to 899cc, then adding a four-into-two pipe, a full fairing and a huge fibreglass seat-tank unit. The result was not cheap, but it was fast.

The Honda factory were unmoved by the small-scale success of these up-market specials but the British importers thought the market too good to miss. Another engineer and ex-racer, Colin Seeley, produced a neat handlebar-faired special, and in 1978 was approached by Honda UK to build a batch of 100 bikes based on the F2 model.

These were loud and red, and housed twin headlamps in a racy full fairing. Tuned with a hot cam, and named the Phil Read Replica in honour of the former world champion racer, the bike was barely lighter than the standard model and not much faster.

At least it looked the part, as did another late-1970s Honda Britain special, the CB750SS. Like the Read Replica, this had a twin-headlamp fairing and a four-into-one, but its white-based paint scheme was more restrained. The semi-official SS was a brave attempt, though a far cry from more recent factory-built exotica such as the gorgeous RC30.

This pair sold alongside each other in a similar fashion to the CB750F and K. Each provided predictable advantages of lightness and agility over its bigger namesake, at the equally predictable expense of a little lost speed. However, both bikes were good for a shade over 110mph (177kph), and, although neither of them ever made anything like the impact of some of Honda's bigger or smaller fours, many riders found them a worthwhile compromise between power, weight and price.

When they were eventually replaced in 1979 it was by one bike, the CB650. The faithful old motor was bored and stroked to 623cc, giving an output of 63bhp at 9,000rpm. The chassis was a modified version of the 550 set-up, with Comstar wheels and twin front discs. Styling was a rather bland half-way house between the 550K and F, with a four-into-two exhaust.

The CB650 was intended to be Honda's answer to the phenomenally popular Kawasaki Z650 but it lacked its character and was also more expensive. Enlarging the engine yet again gave 115mph (185kph) top speed at the expense of the mid-range urge. Although the 650 handled fairly well and proved trouble-free, it didn't really catch on.

Honda found a way to extend their single-cam middleweight four into the 1980s though – the CB650 Nighthawk. Housed in a high-handlebarred custom chassis which lacked the finesse of most contemporary designs, the engine's underwhelming performance was of little consequence in the Nighthawk because cruising at much over 70mph (115kph) was uncomfortable anyway.

That didn't matter to those who valued the bike for its stick-on chrome stripes and a certain amount of laid-back charm. Riders who preferred more up-to-date machinery were less than impressed, though. 'Nightcap' was one of the less offensive nicknames that the CB650SC soon acquired.

Flawed Diamond: The CBX550

In the same way that Honda ended their long line of aircooled 750s by finally producing a twin-cam model, the CBX750, so they had concluded the range of aircooled middleweight fours a year earlier with the introduction of the DOHC CBX550.

Like the CB650 a few years before it, the CBX arrived to take on a successful Kawasaki – in this case the monoshock GPz550 which had recently revitalized the middleweight division. This Honda was a much more handsome challenger, with striking red-white-and-blue paintwork, a sporty riding position and a distinctive four-into-two exhaust whose downpipes were arranged in a curiously attractive three-one-way, one-the-other fashion.

CBX550F2 (1982)	
Engine	Aircooled 16-valve DOHC transverse four
Bore × stroke	59 × 52mm
Capacity	572cc
Comp. ratio	9.5:1
Claimed power	62bhp @ 10,000rpm
Carburation	4 × 32mm Keihin
Gearbox	6-speed
Tyres, front	3.60 × 18in
Rear	4.10 × 18in
Brakes, front	Twin 230mm (9in) enclosed discs
Rear	230mm (9in) disc
Suspension, front	Telescopic, air-assisted
Rear	Pro-Link monoshock, air-assisted
Wheelbase	1,385mm (54.5in)
Weight	196kg (433lb) wet
Fuel capacity	17 litres (3.7 gallons)
Top speed (approx.)	120mph (193kph)
Standing ¼-mile	12.8sec/100mph (160kph)

This time Honda didn't hold back with the specification. The CBX's all-new motor featured not only twin cams but four valves per cylinder, sixteen in all, and produced an impressive 62bhp at 10,000rpm. Lubrication was obviously critical, for an oil cooler was bolted to the twin-downtube frame, and the black stuff needed changing as frequently as every 2,000 miles.

The high-tech attack did not end inside the engine. Sophisticated cycle parts included air-assisted suspension at both ends, with Honda's Pro-Link rising-rate linkage system at the rear. The forks received TRAC anti-dive and also an innovatively enclosed twin-disc front brake arrangement.

The enclosed discs were intended to cure wet-weather brake lag, something that was still giving problems in the early 1980s but by 1982 had already largely been cured by improved pad material. Honda's shrouding merely made inspecting pad wear or removing the front wheel much more difficult, and the brakes worked no better than most others.

Almost everything else about the bike's performance was excellent, though. While not particularly light at 433lb (196kg), it was small and nimble and handled well. A slight edginess at speed was soon accepted by most riders to gain the impressive ease with which the little CBX could be thrown around.

Although the CBX made most of its power above 6,000rpm and needed revving to give of its best, it was fast. It would scream up to about 120mph (195kph), knock off the standing quarter in under 13sec and, if fitted with the optional half-fairing (which made it the F2 model), would cruise happily and comfortably in the 80s all day. Or until the camchain started rattling, for the CBX550 was one of the guilty bikes that helped give Honda such a dubious reputation for reliability in the early 1980s. Early models suffered widespread camchain problems, and filled-in warranty claim forms soon added a sad postscript to the praise that had been heaped on a very sweet little motorcycle.

CB400/4: Mini-Musclebike for the Masses

If there was one bike that the CBX550 resembled, it was the CB400 four that had appeared some seven years earlier and was still fondly remembered by many.

Having produced another winner in 1971, by shrinking their original 750cc superbike to form the CB500, a year later Honda attempted to repeat the dose by going down a further 150cc to create the CB350 four. Soichiro himself thought they'd succeeded, and was so pleased that he declared the new bike the finest, smoothest Honda ever built.

Others weren't so sure. The 350, looking like a smaller-still version of the CB500 but with slightly higher handlebars, handled well and was as smooth as only a four can be. But its engine put out only a peaky 32bhp, and the bike was no quicker even than Honda's own CB350 twin, let alone the much meatier 450. All of which wouldn't have been too bad on its own, but when the CB350 four was launched in the States it cost almost half as much again as the $800 twin. Those figures patently failed to add up, and Honda wisely decided not to offer the bike for sale in Britain.

The CB400's four-into-one exhaust helped give it a unique style.

Europe didn't get a small-bore four until 1975, another three years on, but the wait was worthwhile. A glance at the spec chart suggests just a CB350 with its engine bored out to 408cc, but there was a lot more to the CB400F than that.

Viewed in the metal, the little 400 was clearly the first Honda designed not for the Yanks but specifically for Europe. Its handlebars were flat, its footrests were set

CB400F (1975)

Engine	Aircooled 8-valve SOHC transverse four
Bore × stroke	51 × 50mm
Capacity	408cc
Comp. ratio	9.4:1
Claimed power	37bhp @ 8,500rpm
Carburation	4 × 20mm Keihin
Gearbox	6-speed
Tyres, front	3.00 × 18in
Rear	3.50 × 18in
Brakes, front	267mm (10.5in) discs
Rear	160mm (6.3in) drum
Suspension, front	Telescopic
Rear	Twin shocks with adjustable preload
Wheelbase	1,359mm (53.5in)
Weight	178kg (392lb) wet
Fuel capacity	14 litres (3.1 gallons)
Top speed (approx.)	102mph (164kph)
Standing ¼-mile	14.6sec/85mph (137kph)

The CB400 four was a small-scale superbike for Europe, with neat looks, low bars and plenty of performance.

further back than normal, its styling was uniquely clean. Paintwork came in a choice of simple blue or red, with the words 'Super Sport' on the tank, and four exhaust pipes slanted dramatically down across the engine towards a single silencer.

Sporty looks and words would not have been much good without the performance to back them up. The 400 was no rocketship, its output of 37bhp at 8,500rpm barely giving it

enough go to reach 100mph (160kph), but it could be hustled along pretty rapidly if the revs were kept up. Of the rival two-stroke 400s around in the mid-1970s (Kawasaki's KH400, Suzuki's GT380 and Yamaha's RD400), none could beat it on top speed, and only the Yamaha was quicker in the quarter-mile.

The Honda would cruise happily at 80–85mph (130-137kph), only needing a flick down through the six-speed gearbox for the severest of hills or headwinds. It sounded good, it was economical and it handled pretty well too, holding its line in bends without the wallowing common of Japanese bikes of the day.

The CB400F was relatively expensive, costing about 15 per cent more than the rival two-strokes in Britain, but plenty of riders were happy to pay the extra for its stylish blend of speed, agility and sophistication. The 400F soon proved reliable too, with no major mechanical weakness.

Although it was too sporty for American tastes, the Honda sold by the boatload in Europe and was barely modified for several years. Apart from a colour change, the 1977-model CB400F2's only distinctive features were pillion footrests that mounted solidly instead of being fixed to the swing arm.

By that time though, Honda had introduced their own rival in the bulbous CB400T twin. Faster, better-handling and more comfortable – though infinitely less charismatic – the Dream was also considerably cheaper. Its arrival heralded the beginning of the end for the four, but the CB400F remains one of those rare motorcycles which live long in the memories of most people who have owned one.

Plus Fours:
The CB750 Grows Up

Given the phenomenal success of Kawasaki's Z900 and Z1000 throughout the 1970s, it is perhaps surprising that Honda did not produce a big twin-cam sporting four of their own until the CB750 had been around for a full decade. When the CB900F did belatedly arrive in 1979, it did so at speed.

That the 900 was designed primarily for the European market was obvious from first sight. Clean flowing lines echoed the then current 'Eurostyled' CB250 and 400 Dreams, and the big bike displayed fairly low handlebars, semi-rearset footrests and the words 'Super Sport' on its sidepanels to complete the picture. This machine, Honda proclaimed, owed its inspiration to the all-conquering RCB endurance racers.

In essence it was a combination of the modified frame and sixteen valve aircooled motor of the CB750KZ (the similarly styled 750F would not arrive for another year), with suspension and brakes from Honda's recently released technological *tour de force*, the six-cylinder CBX1000:

The combination was a good one. The 901cc motor revved to 11,000rpm, putting out a maximum of 95bhp at 9,000rpm. Long-stroke dimensions of 64.5 × 69mm kept it respectably narrow and theoretically helped low-down performance, although the smooth-spinning Honda started pumping really hard only at about 7,000rpm.

The 900F's motor made it capable of 130mph (209kph), and – happily – so did its chassis. A four-into-two exhaust,

and the use of plastic for things like the front mudguard, helped keep weight to 512lb (233kg) dry, below that of the 750K. Suspension worked well, with the multi-adjustable shocks giving a well controlled ride if set to their firmest positions.

'The performance steals your attention, and rightly so because it's the star of the show,' said *SuperBike* of

CB900F (1979)	
Engine	Aircooled 16-valve DOHC transverse four
Bore × stroke	64.5 × 69mm
Capacity	901cc
Comp. ratio	8.8:1
Claimed power	95bhp @ 9,000rpm
Carburation	4 × 32mm Keihin
Gearbox	5-speed
Tyres, front	3.25 × 19in
Rear	4.00 × 18in
Brakes, front	Twin 274mm (10.8in) discs
Rear	297mm (11.7in) disc
Suspension, front	Telescopic
Rear	Twin shocks with adjustable preload, compression and rebound damping
Wheelbase	1,516mm (59.7in)
Weight	233kg (512lb) dry
Fuel capacity	20 litres (4.4 gallons)
Top speed (approx.)	130mph (209kph)
Standing ¼-mile	12.1sec/110mph (177kph)

Japanese bikes in general and the CB900 in particular. 'But improving handling characteristics are continually narrowing the gap between top speed and the ability to control that top speed. The frame never betrays its dubious ancestry and complies with the maxim that if you don't notice it working, it's good.'

Bike labelled this the most purposeful machine ever to emerge from the Honda factory. 'With the CB900FZ we have a motorcycle that does most things excellently,

The CB900FZ had Eurostyling, good handling and plenty of speed, but its engine did not take kindly to being revved.

and the rest merely very well,' the magazine's tester said.

Following the bike's German launch he'd been impressed: 'I considered the 900 then to be the nearest a manufacturer had come to producing the Perfect Motorcycle. After a fortnight and hundreds of miles in all weathers on board the machine in England, I've no reason to revise that first, hasty observation.'

Sadly, poor reliability soured the taste somewhat. That old Honda bugbear the camchain was a particular problem, sometimes snapping without warning after as little as 20,000 miles (32,000km). (The camchain and tensioner were modified on later models.) And, when revved hard on the racetrack, the long-stroke motor's conrods were prone to let go with disastrous consequences.

Despite its sporty pretentions – and a fair few production-race wins when it held together – the 900 was really more suited to a grand-touring role. And it moved a step nearer that in 1981, with the introduction of a fully faired version called the 900F2. The extra weight needed a lot of heaving around, but the F2 was a pretty capable all-round motorcycle.

Winning at All Cost: The Superlative CB1100R

If the sporty-looking CB900F was at heart a big softy best suited to fast touring, then there was no doubt about the natural habitat of the gorgeous red-and-white machine that it spawned in 1981. The CB1100R was designed for the racetrack, built to win big long-distance production events in Australia (especially the famous Castrol Six-Hour) and South Africa. As such, it was produced in small numbers and assembled with little regard to cost. In Britain the bike retailed at £3,700, against £2,100 for the 900 and £2,900 for the CBX six. Only 1,000 were made, and only 100 imported to Britain. All were snapped up.

That the CB1100R should prove a peerless roadster was almost a bonus, but it was in a class of its own on the street as well as on the track. The big Honda reached 140mph (225kph) with an ease that made even the CBX look sluggish and its handling was head and shoulders above anything the Japanese had previously produced.

The motor was basically a big-bore version of the 900 lump, with 70×69mm dimensions giving a capacity of 1,062cc. Compression ratio jumped from the 900's 8.8:1 to 10:1, and power leapt a full 21 per cent to 115bhp at 9,000rpm to make this the world's most powerful production motorcycle. Equally importantly, many components – including the conrods – were strengthened in a successful attempt to keep the motor together.

The frame was a beefed-up 900 unit holding similar air-assisted forks; rear shocks were completely new and featured remote reservoirs to prevent the damping fluid overheating under hard use. Brakes were novel, with two-piston floating calipers gripping large twin front discs.

With its big half-fairing, single seat and excellent ground clearance adding further racy touches, the 1100R was pretty well untouchable from the word go. The Rs won race after race, sometimes to the annoyance of spectators, who were bored rigid by the sight and sound of a handful of Hondas whirring round far ahead of the field.

That did not stop Honda from retouching their masterpiece. The next season the 1100R-C arrived with a full fairing (the original bike was prone to slight instability at high speed), pillion seat, uprated forks and wider wheels. The 1983 model, another year on, had metallic paint, an alloy swing arm and even more revised forks. The details

---

CB1100R (1981)

Engine	Aircooled 16-valve DOHC transverse four
Bore × stroke	70×69mm
Capacity	1,062cc
Comp. ratio	10:1
Claimed power	115bhp @ 9,000rpm
Carburation	$4 \times$ CV Mikuni
Gearbox	5-speed
Tyres, front	3.25×19in
Rear	4.00×18in
Brakes, front	Twin 274mm (10.8in) discs
Rear	297mm (11.7in) disc
Suspension, front	Telescopic with air-assistance
Rear	Twin shocks with adjustable preload, compression and rebound damping
Wheelbase	1,488mm (58.6in)
Weight	235kg (518lb) dry
Fuel capacity	26 litres (5.7 gallons)
Top speed (approx.)	140mph (225kph)
Standing ¼-mile	11.5sec/115mph (185kph)

*Ron Haslam (above) and Wayne Gardner were joint
winners of the Streetbike production series in 1982,
when the magnificent CB1100R-C won every
round.*

might have changed, but one thing remained the same: the
CB1100R was still the best.

Revived by Water:
The CBR Line

Just as Honda had previously run into trouble through their
bold – some would say stubborn – decision to stick with a
four-stroke racebike (the NR500) in the face of overwhelming
two-stroke opposition, by 1986 their range of classy

but expensive V4 roadsters was becoming increasingly
isolated.

	CBR600F (1987)	CBR1000F (1987)
Engine	Watercooled 16-valve DOHC transverse four	
Bore × Stroke	63 × 48mm	77 × 53.6mm
Capacity	598cc	998cc
Comp. ratio	11:1	10.5:1
Claimed power	85bhp @ 11,000rpm	133bhp @ 10,000rpm
Carburation	4 × 32mm Keihin	4 × 38mm Keihin
Gearbox	6-speed	6-speed
Tyres, front	110/80 × 17in	110/80 × 17in
Rear	130/80 × 17in	140/80 × 17in
Brakes, front	Twin 276mm (11in) discs	Twin 296mm (11.6in) discs
Rear	276mm (11in) disc	276mm (11in) disc
Suspension, front	Telescopic forks with air-assistance and TRAC anti-drive	
Rear	Pro-Link monoshock with adjustable preload and rebound damping	
Wheelbase	1,410mm (55.5in)	1,500mm (59in)
Weight	182kg (401lb) dry	222kg (488lb) dry
Fuel capacity	16.5 litres (3.6 gallons)	21 litres (4.6 gallons)
Top speed (approx.)	140mph (225kph)	160mph (257kph)
Standing ¼-mile	12sec/115mph (185kph)	11.2sec/ 125mph (200kph)

Kawasaki, in particular, were proving with their GPZ1000 and 600 that in-line fours could be built relatively cheaply and sold in vast numbers. In 1987 the world's biggest bike-building company swallowed its pride and came out with a pair of machines that went straight for Kawasaki's throat.

The most striking aspect of the CBR1000 and CBR600 was the all-enveloping bodywork style common to both models. Every surface was rounded, nothing stuck out to disturb the air-flow, and even the engines were tucked away out of sight so that effort did not have to be wasted in

The streamlined CBR1000, which had an impressive output of 133bhp at 10,000rpm.

making them presentable. Ford had set a trend with their smooth-surfaced Sierra; now Honda was doing the same, and the jelly-mould jokes were dragged out again.

The bodywork was novel but most of the engineering was not. Beneath all the plastic the motors looked as though they could have been built from design sheets drawn up five years earlier and recently rediscovered in a dusty Kawasaki office drawer.

Both used conventional straight-four designs, with heavily oversquare dimensions. Both featured central Hy-Vo camchains working sixteen valves via twin cams and screw-and-locknut tappets. Both had six-speed gearboxes. The bigger version differed in using a gear-driven balancer shaft, and in placing its alternator behind the block to reduce width.

Only watercooling and the lack of size and weight hinted at the CBR motors' modernity. That and the power outputs: 133bhp at 10,000rpm from the 1000; an equally impressive 85bhp at 11,000rpm from the 600 – both figures exceeding Kawasaki's equivalents.

Chassis designs were equally similar and conventional: steel diamond frames, 17in wheels, telescopic forks with TRAC anti-dive, Pro-Link monoshocks, triple disc brakes.

Far from being the new pinnacle of Honda's R&D expertise, the CBRs represented a move towards giving performance at the right price, and at that they succeeded brilliantly. The CBR1000 was a big lump of motorcycle, weighing nearly 500lb (225kg) dry, but it gave a very acceptable mix of solid handling, long-distance comfort, gut-churning acceleration and 160mph (285kph) top speed.

It immediately sold well virtually everywhere, with the

So successful was the CBR600 that its classic design was almost unchanged and still competitive in 1990, three years after its introduction.

notable exception of America, where its release was delayed until 1989 for fear that its sheer speed would spark paranoid politicians to pass anti-motorcycling legislation. By then it was being replaced in other countries by the 1000F-K, which featured a welcome higher screen (the original made high-speed cruising a pain in the neck), a lower and slightly modified engine, new forks and fat radial tyres. The result was an even more competent do-it-all motorcycle.

The CBR600 meanwhile had proved so successful that its only changes in three years were some fresh paint and some mild tuning which brought power to 93bhp. The Honda still needed to be revved above 7,000rpm to give of its best, but it was good for a rock-solid 140mph (225kph). And its fine handling, impressive reliability and willingness to take on anything from commuting to two-up touring made the bike excellent value for money.

For 1991 the smaller CBR was finally revised with a new 100bph engine, uprated cycle parts and restyled bodywork. But the spirit of the 'poor boy's musclebike' remained the same.

4

Big Is Beautiful
The Gold Wing and
CBX1000

GL1000:
The Gold Wing Phenomenon

It took Honda until 1987 to add watercooling to their straight fours with the CBRs. But by then a liquid-cooled four the company had launched in 1975 had long since grown from being a mere motorcycle to become a cult figure, the centrepiece of a world-wide social happening, even the inspiration for a new type of biking.

The GL1000 Gold Wing that was revealed to the public at the Cologne Show in October 1974 was a landmark machine by any standards. Bigger and heavier than anything else on two wheels, it was also faster and more powerful than all but a handful of rivals such as Kawasaki's Z1 and Laverda's triples.

More to the point, the GL1000 boasted a unique flat-four engine, the mid-1970s novelty of watercooling, the con-

venience of shaft drive, an under-seat fuel tank and a host of other features. It was a bold new bike – but in 1975 that was all it was: a motorbike. Only a couple of years later, the Gold Wing had become as much a mobile lifestyle accessory as a motorcycle.

The unfaired, visually engine-dominated but conventionally styled GL1000 was immediately detested by some riders for its size, weight and the very sophistication that Honda had been so keen to provide. The Lead Wing, they sneered. The elephantine motorbike.

But at the same time the bike was adopted, adapted, praised and even worshipped by others to an extent that set it apart from anything previously seen. The Wing's smoothness, comfort and mile-absorbing ability (and to some extent its ostentatious size and obvious expense) made it the target of an increasingly large collection of enthusiasts. Mostly middle-aged and affluent by motorcycling standards

– particularly in America, where Wing-mania has always been strongest – they formed clubs, organized rallies and social events, fitted vast numbers of accessories, and generally turned their motorcycles into rolling extensions of their personalities.

Terms like Wing Nuts (to describe the riders) and Wing Dings (their meetings) soon became part of everyday motorcycling parlance. The bike's popularity spread, and has continued to do so ever since. The two main American Gold Wing clubs, the Gold Wing Road Riders' Association and the Gold Wing Touring Association, are among the largest motorcycle owners' organizations in the world, with branches all over the States.

The annual Wing Ding is an elaborate and lavishly organized affair which attracts thousands of Gold Wings, many of which are ridden for miles across America to attend. As well as the predictable mix of food, entertainment and contests to find the best-looking bikes, there are technical seminars, silly games and scores of accessory stands to be visited.

GL1000 Gold Wing (1975)

Engine	Watercooled 8-valve SOHC transverse flat-four
Bore × stroke	72 × 61.4mm
Capacity	999cc
Comp. ratio	9.2:1
Claimed power	80bhp @ 7,000rpm
Carburation	4 × 32mm Keihin
Gearbox	5-speed
Tyres, front	3.50 × 19in
Rear	4.50 × 17in
Brakes, front	Twin 280mm (11in) discs
Rear	292mm (11.5in) disc
Suspension, front	Telescopic
Rear	Twin rear shocks with adjustable preload
Wheelbase	1,550mm (61in)
Weight	260kg (571lb) dry
Fuel capacity	19 litres (4.2 gallons)
Top speed (approx.)	122mph (196kph)
Standing ¼-mile	13sec/105mph (169kph)

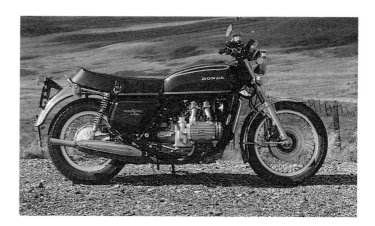

It's easy to forget that when it was introduced the GL1000 Gold Wing looked like an ordinary unfaired motorcycle . . . almost.

The watercooled flat-four engine, shaft-drive system and under-seat petrol tank of the Gold Wing.

There are Gold Wing owners' clubs and groups in numerous other countries too, with rallies, runs and meetings taking place somewhere almost every week of the year. The Gold Wing European Federation is an umbrella organization for the fifteen separate national owners' groups, each of which holds an annual Treffern, as they're normally called in Europe. These don't approach American scale but they are large, well organized events all the same. More than a thousand bikes turned up for the Belgian Treffern near Brussels at Easter 1990.

Needless to say, other manufacturers have noted the Gold Wing's popularity over the years, and have produced rival heavyweight mile-eaters of their own. Some have been good; since the GL's arrival, the best long-distance motorcycle has not always been a Honda. But constant revisions have generally kept the Wing flying up front. And, over the years, no other single bike has come close to inspiring the world-wide loyalty or sense of identity of the Gold Wing riders.

It is doubtful that the possibility of such long-standing hero-worship even occurred to the Honda engineers who met in late 1972 to plan their company's response to bikes such as the Z1 and BMW R90S, which had stolen much of the glory that the CB750 had enjoyed a few years before. They knew the stakes were high, though. The new bike was to be the fastest and finest in the world, the flagship to put Honda back on top.

The new machine was always intended to have a *gran turismo* bias, but early designs included none of the fully faired luxury of today. The first prototype was a 1,470cc flat-six code-named the AOK, fairly similar in appearance to the final bike, but it was abandoned due to the excessive length of its engine. Another prototype resembled a flat-four version of the CB750, with four pipes, single front disc brake and relatively slim styling incorporating a 750-shaped tank, small sidepanels and space round the engine.

But by the time the Gold Wing finally appeared, all attempts to hide its then outrageous dry weight of 570lb (260kg) had seemingly been abandoned. The styling was rounded – 'bulging, pregnant flanks', one reporter commented – the engine was vast, the lack of sporting intent was clear.

The engine capacity had been fixed at a fraction under one litre, from oversquare dimensions of 72 × 61.4mm. The single overhead camshaft at the outside of each pair of watercooled cylinders was driven by a toothed belt running across the front of the motor. The engine breathed in via a cluster of four carbs sitting above the engine, out through a pair of rounded silencers, and produced a claimed maximum of 80bhp at 7,000rpm – enough to drag its bulk up to a top speed of just over 120mph (193kph).

The chassis was conventional in all but scale, comprising a twin-downtube cradle frame, normal telescopic forks and twin rear shocks. The Wing was the first Japanese bike to come with triple disc brakes, but its most notable styling feature was the dummy petrol tank, which hinged open to reveal a limited amount of storage space and the filler cap for the under-seat reservoir.

To say that reactions to the bike were mixed would be like saying that the Gold Wing was a sizeable bike. Predictably, it received its best press in America, where *Cycle* was as impressed by its 12.92sec quarter-mile and its list of features as by any ability to cover big distances:

'If Honda is going to sell a motorcycle for $3,000, then by all that's holy it's going to be worth it. For your dough you get a shaft drive bonus, a triple-disc bonus, a fat rear tire bonus, enough indicator lights to trim a Christmas tree and that final, unexpected, transcendent Extra: except for the Kawasaki 903 Z1, the GL1000 is the hardest-accelerating 1975 production motorcycle you can buy.'

Cycle found little to criticize apart from some transmission snatch, a slightly cramped riding position and a harsh ride over freeway expansion joints. Even handling was rated good: 'The GL's low centre of gravity gives it an extremely responsive feel for a machine that weighs close to 650lb [with fuel]. The only time a rider notices the difference in feel from one of the 750s, which weigh

A more serious flaw of the original Wing was lack of fuel capacity.

about 125lb (55kg) less, is when the big bike is muscled through a series of tight switchback turns. Neither end of the GL oscillates or snakes around alarmingly within the bounds of the bike's ground clearance.'

By no means all British testers agreed. The now defunct magazine *Motorcyclist Illustrated* was pleasantly surprised by the Honda's ability to be thrown around on twisty lanes – 'considering its weight and sheer bulk the Wing performed creditably in an area for which it was obviously not specifically designed' – but was worried by its unease at speed.

'Up to 100mph [160kph] the machine sits there on the road with all the stability one would expect of a heavyweight . . . But at 100mph and over, on that longitudinally ribbed concrete surface which crops up on many roads, the test machine would break into a disconcerting and often downright frightening weave without provocation from raised white lines or cats' eyes.'

In the early 1980s the Wing Nuts had a choice: either buy an Aspencade (left) with Honda's own fairing and luggage, or do it yourself with a fairing from Windjammer or the like (right).

Gold Wing riders, generally older than the average biker, are always keen to show the presentable side of motorcyclists . . .

Blame was aimed at the tyres, and the test was also critical of the suspension, seat and riding position ('all three are not remotely in the BMW class, though by Japanese standards there is little to moan about from the comfort angle'); the brakes, which 'never gave cause for concern, but offered the rider little feedback and required strong pressure from high speed'; and the fuel tank, whose 4.2-gallon (19.1-litre) capacity was pitifully small.

But the tester, Peter Rae, was won over by the Wing's long-legged comfort and its smooth acceleration, and his summary was positive: 'Even with these present limitations, the GL1000 captured my imagination as a desirable and effortless tourer. It just begs to be ridden across a continent, and the next time the opportunity arises I think I'll succumb to that temptation.'

Rae eventually did not only that, but became a Wing owner himself and in 1984 wrote a book called *Gold Wing: An American Japanese Motorcycle* which is still selling now. A very different reaction came from rival magazine *Bike*, whose tester Bill Haylock achieved notoriety (and lost the magazine a year's advertising from the British importers) for his review headlined 'Two-Wheeled Motor Car?'

He too praised the engine's smoothness and effortless power delivery, and the bike's comfort at legal speeds. But he began by questioning the function of a bike that 'reflects Honda's avowed policy of making the motorcycle more socially acceptable and safer, even if it also makes them more boring . . .

'It's an image bike, pure and simple. It ain't meant to be functional – it's just meant to swell your head. It's for the guy who loves spending half an hour every time he stops to fill up, explaining to the impressionable onlookers about how his bike's got four watercooled cylinders, with belt-driven camshafts, and shaft drive . . . an' if you peer in there behind the radiator you can see the cooling fan – just like a car.'

The test also took strong exception to the looks, the fuel range – 80 miles (130km) if the pessimistic gauge was believed or 100-110 miles (160-180km) of fast cruising if not – the handling, the complexity and particularly the weight. 'That superfluous hundredweight and a half [over the R90S] drags down the performance to the level of a good, light 750, negating the Wing's 250cc advantage, and yet you pay the penalty of higher fuel consumption, poor handling and rapid tyre wear . . .

'I can think of several bikes weighing half as much, giving half the power and costing half the price, which are more fun to ride than the Wing. And when it comes down to it, that's what a bike's all about – having fun. And if all the gadgets and gizmos and complexity don't make the Gold Wing any more fun, what's the point?'

The point that Haylock had ignored (among some sharp observations) was that his own idea of fast-and-furious fun, one-up on a nimble but uncomfortable lightweight, differed totally from the laid-back, loaded-up motorcycling that rather a lot of other riders enjoyed.

That was particularly true in America, where as early as 1976 a survey for *Road Rider* found that the average Gold Wing owner was forty years old and covered more than 10,000 miles (16,000km) a year – many of them, no doubt, with a pillion, and some with a trailer tacked on for good measure. The GL1000 soon became hugely successful in the States, selling over 25,000 units a year. Accessory firms quickly latched on to the bike to develop a range of products to improve its seat, its suspension, its handlebars, its acreage of chrome-plate. Almost everything could be personalized to set your bike apart from others at the Wing Ding. And Honda too eventually reacted to develop the basic product and give the big-mileage (or the big-ego) customers something even closer to the machine they desired.

Spreading the Wing: From Aspencade to the Six

At first, Honda's changes were just to details – in the couple of years after its launch, the Gold Wing received a grease-nipple here, a paint job and a little extra chrome there, and also a slightly more comfortable seat.

In 1978 there were more important mods. Smaller carbs, softer valve timing and revised ignition improved the 1,000cc engine's low and mid-range power at the expense of a little top-end. The compromise was welcomed by most riders, for low-rev performance had been relatively weak. The change reflected the fact that, with the recent arrival of Honda's spectacular six-cylinder CBX, the Wing was evolving ever-more into a specialized long-distance tourer.

There were other minor mods that year, too – brighter headlight, comfier stepped seat, Comstar wheels, revised suspension, and brakes that worked a little better in the rain. But in 1979 the Gold Wing was barely touched, and was given a hard time that year by rivals such as Yamaha's XS1100, BMW's R100RT and Kawasaki's vast Z1300.

Honda's reply came in 1980, with the much improved GL1100. The engine was bored out to 1,085cc, improving both power and torque, and its crankshaft and clutch were strengthened. The chassis was also uprated, with a revised frame and all-new air-assisted suspension at both ends.

The result was a much improved motorbike. Even *Super-Bike* magazine, whose professed predilection was for sleek Italian sportsters, was impressed: 'The new engine has just made the Wing a lot nicer to ride. Its earlier incarnations were too peaky. This one combines fair bottom end with plenty at the top, in a civilized and fuss-free combination.

'More big news is the frame and suspension, which have lifted the Wing several rungs up the ladder towards greater versatility . . . By adopting air-suspension front and rear, Honda have made the hippo ride comfortably – at last. Where a freeway bump would have had the last bike first bottoming harshly, then wallowing while trying to recover its poise, and finally weaving disturbingly along a straight piece of road, the new bike just soaks up the bumps.

'It's the wide-open spaces where the Wing excels. And where before it did so only because of its silken engine and abundance of horsepower, it now does so for many other reasons as well. Straight-line stability, comfort and tireless refinement have been added to and reinforced . . . If your life consists of broad highways, it is the one for you.'

Unless, that was, you could afford Honda's big shot of

1980 – the fully dressed version of the 1100, which was known as the Interstate in America and the De Luxe in Europe. After years of sitting back and watching while accessory manufacturers got rich pandering to riders who bought fairings, hard luggage and crashbars for their Gold Wings, Honda finally designed a bike with all those things included as standard – and immediately sold every one they could make.

Two years later came the Aspencade, named after a big American rally dominated by Gold Wing riders. The new bike added to the Interstate the luxuries of a sound system, passenger backrest and an on-board compressor with which to adjust the air suspension.

'Forget the old touring standards; they've been upgraded,' gushed *Cycle*. 'And if you think there's no reason for transcontinental motorcycling, forget that too, because now there's Aspencade. This comfort-cruise missile couches its human cargo in a spacious lounge, and supplies its pilots with an advanced on-board entertainment centre and conveniences no other production motorcycle has ever had.'

With the Aspencade, Honda pushed the Wing yet further towards luxury and social acceptability at the expense of cost and weight – now up to a massive 766lb (347kg) with a full tank of petrol. But, while it would never be the bike for everyone, and was criticized for excessive engine heat, lack of ground clearance and the absence of a throttle cruise control, this was the machine that defined the Gold Wing's role for the foreseeable future.

Even *Bike* was impressed with the Aspencade, its 1983

The six-cylinder GL1500 restored the Gold Wing's performance to original levels, despite all the bulk and weight added over the years.

test rating the bike 'quicker and more agile than its size would suggest', and 'just the kind of sumptuous off-the-shelf intercontinental cruising package Honda's venerable Gold Wing motor has been begging for since 1975.'

But in that year the Aspencade gained a direct rival in Yamaha's XVZ1200 Venture, a smooth V4 with under-seat fuel tank and a similarly lavish level of equipment. And

Bike's next sentence commented that Honda's flat-four motor was 'beginning to show its age. Born in an age when all Japanese motors were at worst very peaky or at best just peaky, even adding 100 cubes to the original mill hasn't bequeathed the sort of effortless bottom-end stomp the rest of the concept suggests.'

Honda's response was to redesign their bike as the GL1200, with not only more power (94bhp at 7,000rpm) and

The GL1500 showing off its flight deck features.

torque but maintenance-free hydraulic tappets and clutch. New frame, suspension, fairing and seat resulted in slight but worthwhile improvements in handling, ground clearance and comfort. The anti-dive system and linked braking arrangement (the foot pedal operating the rear disc and one of the front pair) that had been introduced in 1983 were retained.

The bigger motor, its capacity of 1,182cc reached by increasing the stroke from 61.4 to 66mm and widening the bore a shade to 75.5mm, was undoubtedly a far stronger, punchier motor than the original GL1000 powerplant. The GL1200 continued to sell well, particularly in America. But the change had taken its toll on performance and, with all its extra weight and frontal area, the 1987 Gold Wing was marginally slower than its predecessor of twelve years before.

Finally, Honda had no choice but to abandon the faithful four – and in its place they chose the flat-six layout used in the original AOK prototype and then discarded. The new engine owed much to the fours, notably the watercooled single-cam layout with two valves per cylinder and hydraulic tappets. But the world's largest motorcycle powerplant, its 71×64mm dimensions not far off those of the original 1,000cc motor, put out a much more respectable 100bhp at 5,200rpm with the smoothness that only six cylinders could manage.

With the exception of its cam-covers, the motor was completely hidden behind plastic bodywork which extended from the tip of the front mudguard to the toe of the trunk. If the old Aspencade was a huge bike, then the battleship

GL1500 was positively enormous – almost a metre across its bows, with a wheelbase of 1,700mm (the GL1000's was 150mm shorter) and a claimed dry weight of almost 800lb (365kg), nearer 900lb (410kg) when fuelled up, which made the original 571lb (259kg) Wing seem in need of a cable to stop it blowing away.

Thankfully, one vital difference between the two bikes was that Honda had used the intervening years to develop a chassis that could cope with all that mass. It was stretching a point to say that the new Wing handled well – no bike weighing more than twice as much as Honda's old CB400 four (and even Suzuki's GSX-R750) could claim that. But at least the GL1500 generally went where it was pointed, didn't wobble or weave, and could be cornered as confidently as its bulk would allow.

Equally importantly, the new engine brought performance back above the standards of fifteen years earlier, with much improved low-speed delivery from a powerplant even smoother than the old four. Brush the throttle and the big bike purred quietly and rapidly towards the horizon.

And its ergonomics, predictably, were just as well thought out: big fairing (though the screen was a shade too low for tall riders), sumptuous seat with a generous backrest for the pillion, top-quality luggage and sound systems, cruise control as standard. The starter motor even doubled as an electric reverse gear to help when parking.

What *Bike*'s Bill Haylock would have made of a reverse gear on the original Wing does not bear thinking about. But, as a tester for the same magazine in 1988, I couldn't help

GL1500 Gold Wing	
Engine	Watercooled 12-valve SOHC transverse flat-six
Bore × stroke	71 × 64mm
Capacity	1,520cc
Comp. ratio	9.8:1
Claimed power	100bhp @ 5,200rpm
Carburation	2 × 33mm CV
Gearbox	5-speed
Tyres, front	130/70 × 18in
Rear	160/80 × 16in
Brakes, front	Twin 296mm (11.6in) discs
Rear	296mm (11.6in) disc (linked system)
Suspension, front	Telescopic
Rear	Twin shocks; one coil spring, one air-assisted
Wheelbase	1,700mm (66.9in)
Weight	362kg (796lb) dry
Fuel capacity	23 litres (5.1 gallons)
Top speed (approx.)	125mph (200kph)
Standing ¼-mile	12sec/110mph (177kph)

being impressed by Honda's attention to detail – and more so by the ease with which the giant cycle ate up the miles. Even with all that weight, it was an enjoyable bike to ride.

My main disappointment was that over the years the Gold Wing's price had grown in step with its size. At over £10,000 in Britain in 1990, it cost almost twice as much as Honda's CBR1000. But at least you got a lot of bike for your money. The GL1500 was undoubtedly the best Gold Wing

Some riders have so much luggage that even a GL1500 isn't big enough.

yet, and as a machine for covering many miles in perfect comfort, it was unchallenged. Except, perhaps, by cars of the four-wheeled variety.

The Joy of Six: Honda Fights Back with the Sensual CBX1000

Few motorcyclists in the mid-to-late 1970s would have disagreed with the comment that Honda's range was

becoming rather boring. By 1977 the Gold Wing had been around for a couple of years. Elsewhere in the range, the single-cam CB750s and 550s were based on relatively ancient designs, and the middleweight twins were nothing too inspiring.

The CBX changed all this at a stroke. Visually, technically and audibly stunning – with a unique spine-tingling yowl

CBX1000 (1978)	
Engine	Aircooled 24-valve DOHC transverse six
Bore × stroke	64.5 × 53.4mm
Capacity	1,047cc
Comp. ratio	9.3:1
Claimed power	105bhp @ 9,000rpm
Carburation	6 × 28mm Keihin
Gearbox	5-speed
Tyres, front	3.50 × 19in
Rear	4.25 × 18in
Brakes, front	Twin 276mm (10.75in) discs
Rear	295mm (11.6in) disc
Suspension, front	Telescopic
Rear	Twin shocks with adjustable preload, compression and rebound damping
Wheelbase	1,495mm (59in)
Weight	263kg (580lb) wet
Fuel capacity	20 litres (4.4 gallons)
Top speed (approx.)	135mph (217kph)
Standing ¼-mile	11.7sec/115mph (185kph)

The CBX1000 looks neat and almost like a normal twin-cam Honda four at a side-on glance.

when revved hard – this dynamic bombshell of a motorcycle was launched in 1978 to remind the world of Honda's sporting heritage, and to regain the company's reputation for producing fast, exciting motorcycles.

Not only did the CBX have six cylinders, twenty-four valves, more than 100bhp and a top speed of 140mph (225kph). Equally importantly, the technology was on display in a massive forward-angled bank of aircooled pots from which curved six gleaming downpipes.

Like a heavyweight champion stripped to the waist, the six oozed raw, unashamed power. As a statement of corporate prowess it was unmissable. As a means of restoring Honda's image it was simply magnificent.

All of which would have been of little use had the CBX's inevitable weight and complexity resulted in bad handling and impracticality. Happily, this was not the case. With the Gold Wing around to satisfy touring riders, Honda were free to design the newcomer as a pure sportster. They combined the company's six-cylinder racing experience with some new tricks to ensure that the motor was sweet, and that the handling, while by no means perfect, was at least respectable.

The 1,047cc engine owed a huge debt to Honda's enormously successful multi-cylinder racers of the 1960s, many of which used the four-valve-per-cylinder layout adopted for the CBX. A Hy-Vo chain worked the two-piece exhaust camshaft, with another chain running from that to the inlets. The twenty-four tiny valves were operated by buckets-and-shims.

Angling the cylinder bank forward by 33 degrees allowed the rider some leg room; angling the six carburettors inwards, in two pairs of three, allowed a little more. But the cleverest move was the jackshaft: a chain-driven auxiliary shaft, set above the gearbox, which carried the alternator and ignition system (plus the starter motor), traditionally situated on the end of the crankshaft.

This meant that, despite its six big oversquare cylinders, the CBX engine was only 2in wider than the CB750 four's, allowing a generous amount of ground clearance. The motor was used as a stressed member of a tubular frame, which was designed so that no messy downtubes spoiled the visual effect.

Suspension was conventional, with non-adjustable telescopic forks, multi-variable twin shocks and triple disc brakes. Styling was a mixture of the bold – the block-of-flats-like engine up front – and the sleekly understated, with attractively flowing lines and just a weight-saving pair of silencers.

To continue the boxing simile, the CBX's impact was that of a heavyweight's uppercut to the chin – or, as *Cycle* put it, of 'a cosmic haymaker that caught the state of the art right in the ten-ring and put all the pretenders back where they belonged'. The best-selling American magazine put the bike's photo on its cover above a simple list of numbers: displacement, number of valves and camshafts, claimed power and quarter-mile performance. As well as six cylinders, it had mighty impressive figures elsewhere too.

Thirteen pages of road and racetrack test later, *Cycle*'s conclusion made stirring reading even when allowances were made for the excitement of a new-launch scoop. 'The

Six was not built for pragmatists. It was built for romantics, for people with soft spots in their hearts for mechanical maximum expressions, for people whose specific reasons for motorcycling match the CBX's specific reasons for being built.

'Its European texture is a breakthrough for the Japanese motorcycle industry. Its engine performance is devastating, its high-speed handling and cornering clearance are remarkable, its drive-line character is unflawed and the linear responsiveness of every control and system is unique in all of motorcycling. It cannot be rationally compared to anything on the street, because nothing except a GP road racer is as narrowly committed to high-speed performance.

'It embodies extravagance without vulgarity and high style without pretense – you see muscles and tendons, not chrome and fussiness. It has been designed, not decorated. There is no trashiness in the concept, and none in the execution.

'The CBX is an immensely flattering bike with perfect elegance and total class, and history will rank it with those rare and precious motorcycles which will never, ever be forgotten.'

The engine's performance was most memorable for the way it combined docility with the hardest acceleration yet experienced from a street bike. 'The Six is smooth, uncannily smooth,' said *SuperBike*. 'When it's idling you have to look hard at the tacho to realise the engine's even running because it's so quiet and vibration free. Touch the throttle and raw power comes out in precise, well-mannered increments . . .

'Below 6,000rpm the CBX is mild, almost innocuous, and

Spreading the Work: Honda's Foreign Factories

The CBX1000 and the Gold Wing were two of the first machines to be built at Honda's American plant in Maryville, Ohio, which was set up in 1978 and began producing bikes a year later.

The Ohio Honda factory was by no means the first outside Japan. As long ago as September 1962 the company established an offshoot in Belgium to assemble and sell mopeds in Europe. The plant was opened six months later, with a target of 10,000 bikes a month. In December 1984 the millionth Belgian-built moped rolled off the production line.

Far Eastern countries have also been used for many years. In 1965 the Kwang Yang Industry Co. began building bikes under licence, and a year later the Thai Honda Manufacturing Co. was set up in Thailand's capital, Bangkok.

Production was started in Mexico in 1971, and in Manaus, Brazil, in 1977. The Maryville plant began work a few months after the creation of Honda Manufacturing (Nigeria) Ltd.

In 1987 Honda Italy began building and exporting bikes of their own, too. It is now possible to buy an NS125R built in Italy, a CB450 produced in Brazil and a GL1500 bolted together in Ohio – not to mention cars from Canada, power products from France, bike engines from Pakistan and generators from India.

In mid-1990 it even seemed possible that Honda would move its headquarters to America, due to increasing production costs in Japan caused by the rising value of the yen. After visiting the Ohio plant, president Tadashi Kume said he thought it 'irrelevant where the headquarters is located', and that a move to the States would be feasible.

The CBX engine – high, wide and handsome.

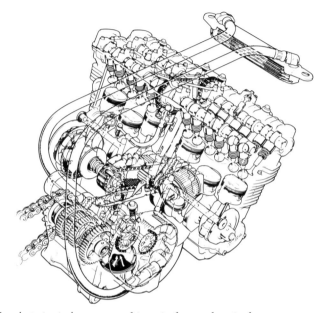

The six pots, twin cams and twenty-four valves took all the glory, but the jackshaft behind the cylinder block was a vital part of the CBX design.

certainly effortless to ride. Above that figure all sorts of things start to happen as it bares its fangs and makes à run for bust.

'Things like the front wheel clawing at the air riding two-up. Things like the sort of acceleration that leaves your shattered reflexes somewhere far behind in the slipstream. Things like the jolt you get in the pit of your stomach as the impossible happens and the bike leaps from 80 to 100mph [130 to 160kph] as if it's doing a fast standing-start quarter.'

But, if the rider planned to make good use of that performance, it was as well to remember that the CBX was not a lightweight racer but a big machine weighing close to 600lb (272kg) with fuel and oil. *Cycle* found it 'virtually impossible to induce wallowing or wobbling in high-speed street cornering', but rated Suzuki's GS1000 four, almost 50lb (23kg) lighter, a better high-speed handler.

Designing Big: Shoichiro Irimajiri

Even the key personnel in Japanese companies such as Honda rarely receive much personal recognition in the West, where the design of a new bike is generally presented as a team effort rather than the work of individuals. One of few engineers to find himself in the spotlight was Shoichiro Irimajiri, who not only led the CBX project but was responsible for several other outstanding Hondas.

The company's policy has traditionally been to let its younger engineers work on racing bikes, while the older hands design the bikes that will be sold to the public. Irimajiri joined Honda in 1963 at the age of twenty-three, and soon became involved in creating some of Honda's legendary race motors: the 250 and 297cc sixes, the 23,000rpm 50cc twin and the jewel-like five-cylinder 125.

Like many of Honda's best engineers, Irimajiri spent time in the late 1960s and early 1970s working on automative products – notably the advanced compound vortex controlled combustion (CVCC) engine announced in 1971. He then followed the path to work on road bikes, and in late 1972 led the team that set out to produce what he told them should be 'the king of motorcycles' – the project which two years later (under the leadership of another engineer, Toshio Nozue) was to result in the launch of the Gold Wing.

By that time Irimajiri had been appointed chief engineer of Honda's Research and Development branch; shortly after that he was involved in the design of the CX500. But it was for his leadership of the CBX1000 project that he became best known.

'When we were racing, we were up against the four-cylinder two-strokes built by Yamaha and Suzuki,' he told *Cycle* magazine at the CBX's launch in 1977. 'Cylinder multiplication was the only way we could be competitive. That's why we built the five and the two sixes. The CBX Six is a direct descendant of those race engines. That's one reason its design only took a year and a half – we had the engine technology from our GP racing experience.'

As is common in Japanese corporations, Irimajiri stayed with Honda and progressed through the ranks. In 1982 he was made the president of HRC, the racing division; then managing director of Honda Motor Co. In June 1989 he took another step up the corporate ladder to become Senior Managing and Representative Director. But you can bet he still remembers the wail of those six-cylinder racers . . .

Bike experienced some alarming instability during flat-out speed-testing on a bumpy track, and questioned the rear shock absorbers, though in normal road use they found little concerning the six's handling to complain about. But *SuperBike* was far less happy, finding that 'at about 130mph [209kph] on a smoothish surface, the front end on our test machine became skittish and started to wander, while high-speed cornering gave me the feeling that the bike was trying to tie knots in itself'.

The discrepancies probably relate to a sensitivity to rear-tyre wear especially typical of bikes of that late-1970s period, when Japanese suspension design was starting to catch up with their engines but tyre technology was lagging behind. By the time the magazine came to pit the six against a 438bhp Aston Martin V8 Vantage in a self-styled Heavy-weight Championship of the World, its rear Dunlop cover was three-quarters worn and resulted in a weave that even former world champion Phil Read, hired as rider for the occasion, could not overcome.

But the bike still outdid the ten times costlier car, driven by another former champ, Derek Bell, in most performance tests. And Read was by no means the only rider to be hugely impressed by the CBX1000's addictive blend of speed and soul.

'It's a much-needed boost for Honda and bikes in general, for it shows that exciting, thrilling, glamorous motorcycles can still be made in Japan,' said *Bike*, who admitted that their pre-test view of a pointless and irrelevant demonstration of muscle-flexing could not have been further from the truth. 'The CBX was quite simply a marvellous revelation which has genuinely elevated the status of motorcycling.'

SuperBike joined in the praise: 'Quite simply there's never been a bike like the CBX. With singleminded dedication, Honda set out to build a prestige roadburner; the world's number one bike from the world's number one manufacturer. It would be churlish to deny that they've succeeded handsomely.'

Softening the Six:
The CBX1000-B

Unfortunately for Honda, the old truism that says a great motorcycle will not always sell in equally great numbers could have been dreamt up just for the CBX. The six's

monumental technical achievement was followed by disappointment in the showrooms, particularly in the all-important American market traditionally dominated by cruisers and tourers.

Honda's answer was to soften the appeal of the monster. In 1981 it gained a fairing, Pro-Link single-shock suspension (at the expense of a 40mm longer wheelbase), uprated brakes and air-assisted suspension at both ends. Not to mention optional panniers – *panniers* on the mighty CBX!

Although the fully-faired CBX1000-B kept the engine on show, the six lost much of its appeal as a tourer.

The conversion to a sports tourer was done fairly efficiently. The fairing gave good protection (barely any plastic was needed at the bottom, given the width of those cylinders), though the low screen left a tall rider's head in the breeze.

The engine, detuned slightly to 100bhp, was as smooth as ever; the new brakes were good; the luggage undeniably useful. The bike, as *Cycle* put it, was 'better shaped and toned and curried and softened for the clientele who could afford a CBX'.

But the new model had none of the raw, brash appeal of the original six, and it was marred by a number of faults in addition to its inescapable bulk and weight. When the weather was hot, the unventilated fairing directed the big engine's heat straight up at the rider; when the pace was hot, the rear shock lost its damping and sent the handling to pieces; and when the journey was long, the seat became very uncomfortable.

In 1982 *Bike*'s tester rode the faired CBX the length of France, and rated it less well suited to the trip than the likes of BMW's R100RS, Moto Guzzi's Spada and Honda's own Gold Wing. Meanwhile, the arrival of newer and faster sports rivals from Kawasaki and Suzuki had left it short on performance.

'The CBX, once the ultimate, has been put firmly in its place by the big GPzs and Katanas,' he concluded. 'Trying to turn it into a tourer has done nothing for it except induce a severe identity crisis.' But the shift in emphasis was at least partially successful, and in the States the softer CBX sold in greater numbers than its flashier forebear.

The bike's unique appeal has resulted in long-standing interest, too. In recent years values have risen, and a CBX owners' club has been established. Based in Texas, the club has over a thousand members, and branches as far apart as Britain, Cyprus and Scandinavia. The CBX might have disappointed in some ways, but nobody could deny the impact it made.

5

Vive la Différence:

Honda Turns to the V4

Concept and Execution:
The VF750S

The idea was so brilliant that people wondered why a bike manufacturer had not produced it already, why Honda had taken thirteen years from the CB750's launch to come up with this earth-shattering new engine design. The VF750S that was launched in 1982 contained a motor so neat, so clever, so obviously *right* for a motorcycle that it looked as though it might lead bikes away from in-line fours for good.

The watercooled 90-degree V4 powerplant built for the VF appeared to have it all. Much narrower than an in-line four of similar size, it also allowed weight to be kept low by arranging the front pair of cylinders almost horizontally.

Other firms – Brough and Matchless, for example – had built bikes around V4s years earlier, but these had been narrow-angle aircooled engines. The 90-degree Honda's perfect primary balance (the crankshaft was arranged at 360 degrees, with each pair of pistons moving together) left

only minor vibration, which could easily be damped out to give a supremely smooth ride. A water-jacket removed any problems in cooling the rear cylinders, and there was enough space in the crook of the V for carburettors. What could be more natural?

This was the first modern V4, and the 748cc engine, its dimensions very oversquare at 70×48.6mm (which helped keep down length – one potential disadvantage of the layout), combined four-valve-per-cylinder technology with efficient intake design to produce a 79bhp unit, which was universally praised for its silky, free-revving power available virtually from idle to red line.

The first mistake that came to light was the motorcycle in which Honda chose to debut their new marvel. Not so much the model aimed specifically at the States, a custom-styled cruiser with long forks, high handlebars, a stepped seat and old-fashioned twin shocks. The V45 Magna (750cc is 45cu in) was a harmless enough waste of the powerplant.

The serious V4 was the bike the Americans called the

VF750S (1982)

Engine	Watercooled 16-valve DOHC 90-degree in-line V4
Bore × stroke	70 × 48.6mm
Capacity	748cc
Comp. ratio	10.5:1
Claimed power	79bhp @ 9,500rpm
Carburation	4 × 32mm Keihin
Gearbox	6-speed
Tyres, front	110/90 × 18in
Rear	130/90 × 17in
Brakes, front	Twin 276mm (10.8in) discs
Rear	160mm (6.3in) sls drum
Suspension, front	Telescopic with air-assistance and TRAC anti-dive
Rear	Pro-Link monoshock with air-assistance and adjustable rebound damping
Wheelbase	1,550mm (61in)
Weight	237kg (522lb) wet
Fuel capacity	18 litres (4 gallons)
Top speed (approx.)	120mph (193kph)
Standing ¼-mile	12.5sec/105mph (169kph)

The VF750S, a case of nice engine, shame about the bike. Then the engine started going wrong.

V45 Sabre – the duelling sword – and others called the VF750S. This placed the new motor in a smart, sophisticated package of high-tech features and cycle parts – Pro-Link single-shock rear suspension, TRAC anti-dive, four-piston brakes, and an enormous electronic instrument console, complete with stopwatch and liquid-crystal warning lights, looking like something from the command deck of the Starship Enterprise.

The whole bike was big and quite heavy, weighing well over 500lb (225kg) with fuel, and few riders took long to decide that one thing the 750S was *not* was a sports bike. High bars meant that using the mildly disappointing 120mph (193kph) top-speed performance for any length of time was impossible, but a more serious problem was the shaft-drive bike's disturbingly vague handling.

Bike magazine was typically blunt. 'You're right. It

doesn't handle,' began their test, which went on to reveal that after one hard, wallowing ride the rear shock – sheltered behind the engine, and worked hard by the Pro-Link system's rising-rate linkages – had been far too hot to touch and had lost all its damping.

The VF did not impress the magazine even at lower speeds, where its smooth engine, shaft drive and tunable suspension might have resulted in a good long-distance machine. Kawasaki's simpler, better-handling and cheaper GT750, ironically an aircooled transverse four, was rated by far the better tourer.

The VF750S's chassis had spoilt what could have been an exceptional motorcycle, and most testers expressed disappointment with the bike as a whole. But all were sure that the world had not heard the last of Honda's VF750 engine. In that respect they were all too literally right.

Fast But Fragile: The VF750F

Only a year after the 750S, Honda introduced the V4 that many thought they should have built in the first place. The VF750F's engine was a chain-drive version of the original V, uprated slightly and with the old bike's overdrive sixth gear removed. It put out an impressive claimed maximum of 90bhp at 10,000rpm.

More importantly, this time the motor was housed in a real sports bike whose chassis was capable of doing it justice. The frame was new, made from box-section steel instead of round tubes like the S-bike, and painted silver to

look like aluminium alloy. Strong members ran from the steering head to the pivot for the swing arm, which really was made of alloy.

Suspension was again air-assisted at both ends, but this time there was not only more damping adjustment but a

VF750F (1983)	
Engine	Watercooled 16-valve DOHC 90-degree in-line V4
Bore × stroke	70 × 48.6mm
Capacity	748cc
Comp. ratio	10.5:1
Claimed power	90bhp @ 10,000rpm
Carburation	4 × 32mm Keihin
Gearbox	5-speed
Tyres, front	120/80 × 16in
Rear	130/80 × 18in
Brakes, front	Twin 280mm (11in) discs
Rear	280mm (11in) disc
Suspension, front	Telescopic with air-assistance, TRAC anti-dive and adjustable rebound damping
Rear	Pro-Link monoshock with air-assistance and adjustable rebound damping
Wheelbase	1,495mm (58.9in)
Weight	231kg (510lb) wet
Fuel capacity	22 litres (4.8 gallons)
Top speed (approx.)	125mph (200kph)
Standing ¼-mile	12sec/110mph (177kph)

decent amount of damping to start with. The TRAC anti-dive stayed, now working in conjunction with the 1983 season's racing-inspired fashion of a 16in front wheel. (The small diameter theoretically allows quicker changes of direction due to reduced inertia, at the expense of reduced stability and extra reaction to bumps.)

Styling was dramatically up-rated, too – racy red-and-white paint, a useful top-half fairing, a belly-pan useful only for displaying a 'V-Four' logo, and generally neat, aggressive lines. Flattish clip-on handlebars leaned the rider forward towards a simple cockpit that looked particularly lean and attractive after the excesses of the 750S.

Best of all, the chassis worked as well as the engine. The VF charged up to a top whack approaching 130mph (209kph) in a typically lazy, free-flowing V4 manner, with healthy acceleration available almost whatever the revs and with barely any vibration. And, where its predecessor had wallowed and lurched, the tall 750F (called the Interceptor in the States) was stable, well balanced and delightfully nimble.

The VF immediately became a best-seller, but before long the nasty rumours about its top-end problems started. Honda initially denied everything, blaming poor servicing when confronted with reports of rapid camshaft wear. They must have been especially horrified to find that their new star of an engine was letting them down.

But disgrace them it did. Early V4s had a poor oil supply to the top end, which caused trouble until modified with a new banjo-bolt. But the longer-lasting malaise was caused by its camshaft design. Valve pressure from one side of the engine frequently loaded the other side when the tappets were being checked, which led to the setting of excessively large valve clearances, and in turn to very expensive noises.

Even after the problem was completely cured (with a special tool which held down the cam while clearances were checked), the ill-feeling lingered. In Britain the importers doubled their engine warranty to two years, but it would take many more months for the motorcycling public to recover their faith.

The irony must have been particularly bitter for the engineers who designed the landmark V4 motor and belatedly created the cycle fit to hold it. The VF750F's Achilles heel sours the memory of what in most respects was a brilliant bike.

V for Variety:
From VF400 to VF1000R

In the early-1980s boom period, when few motorcycle dealers realized that the lines on their sales charts were about to disappear over the edge of a cliff, Honda appeared to be trying to cater for everyone by building engines in a huge variety of configurations. In 1983 their British range included everything from the transverse-six CBX, through straight-fours and V-twins to parallel twins and the big-single FT500.

But the company's heart, it seemed, was in V4s. Along with the VF750F in 1983 came the little VF400F, and a year later the range was further widened by the arrival of the VF500 and a pair of full-litre V4s. This, Honda still seemed to be saying, is the future for motorcycles.

The 400F was a smart-looking little bike, with a handlebar fairing, belly-pan and a shrunken dose of all the things that made the 750F so sweet to ride. Its 399cc sixteen valve

Fast, light and fine-handling, the VF500 was a brilliant little bike, if an expensive one.

motor produced a claimed 53bhp at a worryingly high 11,500rpm, but turned out to have none of the 750's problems. Although it had to be revved hard to make quick progress, the eager 400 was as refreshingly smooth and tractable as its bigger brother. Top speed was around 110mph (177kph), if anything fractionally faster than Yamaha's new middleweight performance yardstick, the power-valve-equipped RD350LC (though the Honda was slightly slower off the line). And the VF's chassis, comprising a steel-tube frame, air-assisted suspension, 16in front wheel, and fussy VT500-style enclosed front disc brake, gave the little bike near-unbeatable handling.

The same was true of the VF500, which appeared a year later boasting not only an extra 17bhp (up to a claimed 70bhp, which proved a shade optimistic) from its bored-and-stroked 498cc engine, but also longer service intervals, normal twin discs and a full fairing that made it look even more handsome. The 500 was more expensive again, and several owners unfortunate enough to crash one were shocked to discover that its fairing alone cost more than a third of the price of the complete bike. There were early reports of reliability problems, too, reportedly due to a batch of faulty crankshafts.

Apart from that, though, the VF500 was a gem. Its motor combined 120mph (193kph) top speed with typically sweet V4 delivery; its handling was as good as the VF400's (although the rear shock's damping deteriorated with time), and its brakes were better.

Honda's attempt to transfer the V4 concept to larger-capacity machinery was less of a success, though that was

Power Games: Honda's Engine Layouts, from Singles to Sixes

Engines have always been at the heart of Honda's technology, not only physically but in spirit. From Soichiro's first 1bhp bicycle add-on to turbocharged F1 race-car power plants putting out 1,000bhp, motors have been the dominant features of the company's products.

No surprise, then, that over the years Honda have used a wide variety of engine layouts in their motorcycles alone: from the earliest two-stroke single to the ST1100, which unlike previous V4 Hondas has a transverse engine, its crankshaft running along the line of the bike.

Honda's reputation was constructed round motors with two or more cylinders placed across the frame. The first parallel twin was the C70 in 1957; the CB750 four was revealed in 1968; and the six-cylinder CBX1000 roadster hit the road a decade after that.

The race department had unleashed their six-pot 250 back in 1964, and a year later produced a fabulous five-cylinder 125cc racer. Both won their respective world championships in 1966. For the next season the factory built a three-cylinder 50cc engine, but they then abandoned the class and it was not raced. Honda have never produced three- or five-cylinder in-line engines for road use.

They did race a V3 two-stroke to good effect in 1983, when Freddie Spencer became world champion on the NS500. They also produced a roadster version, the NS400, the engine of which differed in that its cylinders were arranged two horizontal, one vertical – the opposite of the racer's layout.

Twin-cylinder engines have appeared in various forms, notably the transverse V-twin line starting with the CX500, and the in-line V-twins that lead back to the VT500. Much earlier there was the flat-twin Juno a 125cc scooter built in 1960, and the tandem-twin Liner, a copy of a British Sunbeam. Unlike the flat-four Gold Wing which arrived much later, neither model was sold in Britain.

Most of Honda's many V4s have been four-strokes, the VFs and VFRs. The most powerful was the two-stroke NSR500 factory race bike, introduced in 1984 and still winning races – in much-developed form – in the 1990s. And the most recent was another four-stroke, the ST1100, unveiled in 1989. No doubt there are plenty more new designs where those came from.

no fault of the engine. By enlarging the 750cc motor's dimensions to 77×53.6mm they brought capacity up to 998cc, which with bigger carbs and valves, hotter cam-shafts and new pipes, helped give the VF1000F a claimed 116bhp at 10,000rpm.

The rest of the bike was virtually identical to the VF750F, from its square-section steel frame (forks were slightly thicker) to its distinctive bodywork, comprising top-half fairing and belly-pan.

The family resemblance was beneficial in a practical way, for the tall, narrow-feeling VF was as easy to steer as the 750, and stable right up to its new top speed of a shade over 140mph (225kph). The engine was all that could have been hoped for. It produced beautiful streams of free-flowing V4

*The VF1000R should have been the race-winning V4
that put the 1000F in the background, but the R was
far too heavy as well as too expensive.*

VF1000R (1984)

Engine	Watercooled 16-valve DOHC 90-degree in-line V4
Bore × stroke	77 × 53.6mm
Capacity	998cc
Comp. ratio	11:1
Claimed power	122bhp @ 10,000rpm
Carburation	4 × 36mm Keihin
Gearbox	5-speed
Tyres, front	120/80 × 16in
Rear	140/80 × 17in
Brakes, front	Twin 275mm (10.8in) discs
Rear	215mm (8.5in) disc
Suspension, front	Telescopic with air-assistance and anti-dive
Rear	Pro-Link monoshock with adjustable rebound damping
Wheelbase	1,505mm (59.2in)
Weight	238kg (524lb) dry
Fuel capacity	25 litres (5.5 gallons)
Top speed (approx.)	150mph (241kph)
Standing ¼-mile	11.5sec/125mph (200kph)

horsepower whatever the revs, with enough bottom-end to pull away smoothly around town and enough mid-range urge to wrench the pilot's arms from their sockets when the throttle was cracked open.

Unfortunately, the 1000F's similarity to the 750 was probably its main weakness too. For the bigger bike failed to stand out from the crowd, and it inevitably suffered from unjust doubts concerning its reliability. It also had two big problems – Kawasaki's GPz900 Ninja and Yamaha's FJ1100, two outstanding rivals which had both been launched at the same time. The VF1000F was a good bike, but in that company it was not quite good enough.

Nor, more surprisingly, was its sharp-suited cousin the limited-edition VF1000R. This red-white-and-blue rocket-ship was to be the showpiece of Honda's range, the V4 equivalent of the all-conquering CB1100R of a few years earlier.

The 1000R looked stunning, its specification was mouth-watering and the quality of its detail work was superb: quick-release front wheel with fully-floating brake discs, carbon-fibre-reinforced full fairing carrying aluminium radiator and rubber-mounted instruments, beautiful forged dural footrests, ventilated rear disc – and at the heart of the bike a tuned version of the 1,000cc V4, driving its camshafts not with chains but with gears (which reduced friction losses and increased valve control at high revs), and producing a claimed 122bhp at 10,000rpm.

But whereas the old aircooled CB1100R had lived up to its price and promise in terms of performance and results, the watercooled litre bike barely hit the racetrack, let alone the winner's circle. Even Honda's rising star, Wayne Gardner, just failed to take what he disloyally described as a marshmallow to victory in the prestigious Castrol Six-Hour production race in Australia. When it came to paying to race the V4 there were understandably few takers.

Weight was the VF1000R's problem, both in absolute terms – at 524lb (238kg) dry it was more than 50lb (23kg) heavier than Kawasaki's GPz900R, the production racers' favourite – and in the surprisingly ponderous, top-heavy feel of its handling. The Honda was typically torquey, well braked and reassuringly stable all the way to its 150mph (241kph)-plus top speed, but despite its 16in wheel the so-called racer was harder to pull into a tight bend than the humble 1000F.

The VF1000R cost over £5,000 in Britain in 1984, almost half as much again as the F model. That price put it on par with the genuine exotica being hand-produced by firms such as Bimota and Harris. The R was simply not in the same league, and Honda were doubtless relieved that they had planned to build only a limited number.

If the VF1000R had a forte it was not as a racer but as a flashy long-distance road burner – albeit for the rich type whose only luggage was a gold credit card. The VF1000F, too, had failed to match the opposition for performance so Honda chose to soften it in much the same way they had the CBX1000.

The VF1000F2 Bol d'Or was a passable attempt to make a sports tourer out of a bike that could no longer cut it as a sportster.

In 1985 the big V was treated to a full fairing painted in subdued grey, an 18in front wheel to replace the 16in wheel for slower steering, and revised geometry with slightly less steep forks for the same reason.

The result was called the VF1000F2 Bol d'Or, after the famous 24hr race in the south of France, but the name turned out to be an inappropriate choice. The rather ungainly Bol d'Or was less suited to a racetrack than its predecessor, the VF1000F, although a fearless Isle of Man expert named Geoff Johnson somehow managed to beat the Kawasakis to win that year's Production TT on one.

When it came to travelling the length of France to spectate at the Bol, that old CBX failing – the uncomfortable seat – prevented the F2 from fulfilling the big V4 unit's considerable potential as a sports-touring powerplant. For an afterthought the fairing was a fair attempt, but its screen was too low and the newly shrouded engine was prone to overheating.

That apart, the big Honda did nothing particularly badly but nothing especially well. This time, though, there was no six-cylinder CBX charisma to save its embarrassment in the showroom.

VFR750: Taking the Fast Road Back

The VFR750 was not just an important motorcycle for Honda, it was a vital one. In 1986 the world's biggest bike company was suffering badly, not only in the aftermath of

The VFR750 was a bike with a lot of pressure on its shoulders. Happily for Honda, it could take the strain.

the VF750's much publicized unreliability, but also from the excellence of recently released rivals such as Suzuki's oilcooled GSX-R750 – ultra-light and racy – and Yamaha's watercooled FZ750, with its twenty valves and mightily strong mid-range power.

Honda's big-bike range – comprising the VFs, the end-of-the-line aircooled CBX750 and the perennial Gold Wing – was dated and uninspiring by comparison. The VFR arrived to find the spotlight shining right in its face: the new bike had to be exceptionally good, and it had to be impeccably reliable.

It was. To produce the VFR750, Honda's engineers took the logical approach, redesigning the VF750F with the benefit of three years' experience to arrive at a bike that was lighter, lower, more powerful and mechanically stronger than its forebear.

Much of the weight-saving – at 436lb (198kg) dry, the newcomer was lighter by 57lb (26kg) – came from the adoption of a frame which combined an aluminium main spine, using the engine as a stressed member, with a detachable steel rear subframe. In the fashion popularized by Suzuki with their GSX-Rs, the Honda used extruded alloy for the rectangular-section main rails, and cast lumps for the complicated shapes at the steering head and swing-arm pivot.

Cycle parts such as the forks and front brake calipers were correspondingly reduced in size to save more weight, the latter with the aid of innovative ceramic-backed pads for increased heat insulation. The front wheel remained 16in in diameter. Forks were air-assisted; the single rear shock was adjustable by means of an easily used hydraulic knob behind a sidepanel.

The watercooled motor kept the old VF's oversquare 70 × 48.6mm bore and stroke and even its 10.5:1 compressions ratio, relying on improved efficiency and lighter pistons, conrods and valves for its extra power – output was up 15bhp to a claimed 105bhp at 10,500rpm.

Camshafts were turned by VF1000R-style gears instead of by chains, and a 180-degree crankshaft replaced the VF's 360-degree arrangement, the paired pistons now moving in opposite directions. (Honda said the 180-degree engine gave smoother, more regular firing intervals but the main improvement was arguably its sharper exhaust note.)

The VF's roomy feel and fairly upright riding position were retained, although the new model was significantly lower and aerodynamically more efficient. In its sober

VFR750 (1986)

Engine	Watercooled 16-valve DOHC 90-degree in-line V4
Bore × stroke	70 × 48.6mm
Capacity	748cc
Comp. ratio	10.5:1
Claimed power	105bhp @ 10,500rpm
Carburation	4 × 34mm Keihin
Gearbox	6-speed
Tyres, front	110/90 × 16in
Rear	130/80 × 18in
Brakes, front	Twin 276mm (10.9in) discs
Rear	256mm (10in) disc
Suspension, front	Telescopic with air-assistance
Rear	Pro-Link monoshock with adjustable preload
Wheelbase	1,480mm (58in)
Weight	198kg (436lb) dry
Fuel capacity	20 litres (4.4 gallons)
Top speed (approx.)	145mph (233kph)
Standing ¼-mile	11.8sec/120mph (193kph)

plastic suit of pearl-white or dark blue (in America, the VFR750 Interceptor wore brighter clothes), the bike was intended as an 'exciting yet mature' all-rounder, Honda announced, rather than a race replica like the Suzuki GSX-R750. But in Britain, at least, its initial sales success was ensured on the track.

Honda UK had no machine for their Grand Prix star Ron Haslam to ride in the annual Britain-against-America match race series at Easter, and persuaded him to line up on a standard VFR750 against a gridful of international aces on real race bikes. Haslam's third place in one televised leg was due more to his inspired riding in the rain than the

In 1990 the VFR750F became sportier, with sleeker looks, stiffer frame and firmer suspension.

roadster's suitability for the job but the importers cared little. Two days later their entire year's allocation of VFR750s had been sold.

Equally importantly, the VFR750 won praise from just about everyone who rode it for its blend of performance and practicality. The Honda was comfortable enough for commuting or touring, yet at the same time it was fast enough to keep up with its 750cc rivals anywhere other than on a racetrack – and it wasn't far behind even there.

Suspension at both ends was very adequate, and the VFR's handling managed to combine quick steering with a rock-steady feel all the way to a top speed not far short of 150mph (241kph). And if the V4's top-end power was impressive, its low and mid-range delivery was even better: open the throttle and an instant, step-free gathering of momentum sent the bike scuttling smoothly along as though powered by an enormous elastic band.

When the pressure had been on, Honda had come up with the goods. The VFR750 was a triumph, for the feel of its engine and for its unparalleled versatility as a roadster.

Two years later, in 1988, the VFR was updated with a modified screen and fairing (complete with clock and fuel gauge), new suspension, bigger brakes, 17in wheels at both ends, and a little more power from increased compression ratio, bigger valves and a reworked exhaust system. Though the new front forks were on the soft side, the other changes – especially the screen, which could be hinged upwards to give extra wind protection – all contributed to making the VFR even better.

In 1990 the bike changed much more dramatically, while

keeping a broadly similar appearance. Nearly every component was subtly redesigned, seemingly in an atttempt to make the VFR a little more aggressive and to give it some extra flash and handling prowess with which to counter the appeal of brighter-painted tackle such as Kawasaki's popular ZXR750.

Engine changes were aimed largely at making the powerplant more compact, so that it could be moved forward and downwards in the chassis to improve weight distribution. The original Honda V4 method of rocker-arm valve adjustment was changed to a bucket-and-shim layout, which is more compact (servicing is more complicated, but intervals were tripled to 22,000 miles (35,000km)), and the valve angle was steepened to reduce width further. Other changes included larger carburettors and a strengthened crankshaft, but rather than making more power the new motor's peak output of 100bhp at 10,000rpm was slightly down. Mid-range response, though, was stronger than ever.

The smaller engine was bolted into an all-new aluminium frame which used not one but two extruded rails on each side. Crucial chassis dimensions such as wheelbase and steering angle were reduced, and the rider joined the motor in being shifted slightly lower in the machine. Suspension was revamped, wheels were widened, and the swing arm was changed to the race-developed (but heavier) single-sided Pro-Arm.

The revamped VFR was still a great all-round motorcycle, albeit one which was slightly more narrowly focused than before. Although some aspects such as the suspension and headlamp were improved, the lower screen was less effective and the fuel tank was smaller. And the changes had cost pounds, both in weight – the new bike was 30lb (13.5kg) heavier – and in price, for the VFR was the most expensive of the 750cc roadsters, and sold for almost as much as Honda's simpler in-line four, the CBR1000.

Those old enemies, complexity and expense of production, had ensured that Honda's V4s would not prove to be the face of motorcycling's future after all. But the VFR750 had salvaged Honda's reputation, and it entered the 1990s as competent, as full of character and as distinctive a bike as ever.

Road Racer:
The Astonishing RC30

Those three descriptions were even more true of the remarkable V4 motorcycle that Honda had produced two years earlier, not so much as a development of the VFR750F roadster but as a direct spin-off from the RVF750 factory racers which had dominated four-stroke competition to an almost tedious degree in the preceding few years.

The VFR750R, code-named the RC30, was more than just a homologation special like Honda's CB1100R and VF1000R of the past. It was more, too, than an evocative race-replica such as the updated Suzuki GSX-R750 which was released at the same time, and which tempered its factory-bike appearance with road-riding concessions including a dual seat and roadster gearbox.

The RC30 was the real thing – or as close as had yet been seen on the road. Its looks copied the all-conquering race

The RC30 was based to an unprecedented degree on the all-conquering RVF750 factory race bike.

The French pairing of Gerard Coudray (above) and Patrick Igoa retained Honda's endurance world title in 1985 on the mighty RVF750.

bike to an unprecedented degree, from its tiny dimensions and twin-headlamp fairing to its alloy frame, which was rumoured to be cast in the same die as the RVF's, to its single-sided swing arm, pioneered by ELF and successfully used on Honda's works endurance racers to speed wheel changes.

The roadster's seat unit, like the racer's, was a single moulding with a couple of pieces of foam glued on for 'comfort'; there was no room for a pillion. Tachometer and

temperature gauge were foam-mounted; the speedometer and warning lights, unnecessary on the track, were separate for easy removal. Handlebars, footrests, petrol tank and rear subframe were all made from aluminium, the latter a bolt-on addition to the massively strong main twin-beam structure.

Forks were also supremely strong, their 43mm diameters identical to the RVF's, as were those of the 310mm-wide floating disc brakes. Both forks and the remote-reservoir rear shock unit could be fine-tuned for both compression and rebound damping.

Honda claimed that the single-sided Pro-Arm was more rigid than a conventional swing arm of similar weight. Although few experts believed them (simple physics suggested that twisting forces would add load and require extra strengthening), the unique right-side view of an apparently unsuspended white rear wheel was undeniably striking.

The RC30's motor was as exotic as its rolling chassis. Basically a tuned, slimmed-down version of the standard VFR lump, it used a 360-degree crankshaft, like the old VF design (and also the RVF racers), as this had been found to give better drive out of corners than the 180-degree VFR750F arrangement.

Not surprisingly, most of the RC30's numbers were impressive. Peak horsepower was a claimed 112bhp at 11,000rpm, 7bhp up on the F-model; dry weight, at 407lb (185kg), was about 30lb (14.5kg) lower; wheelbase was a

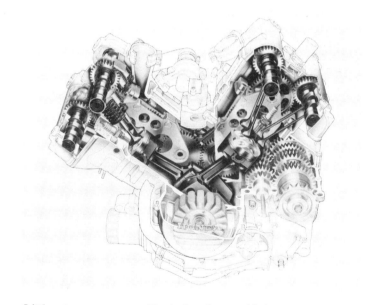

The single-sided Pro Arm swing-arm fitted to the VFR400 and RC30 was developed for endurance racing, where quick wheel changes are all-important.

Little expense was spared in the hand-assembled RC30 engine which featured a 360-degree crankshaft, titanium conrods, and an 80mph (130kph) first gear.

VFR750R (1986)

Engine	Watercooled 16-valve DOHC 90-degree in-line V4
Bore × stroke	70 × 48.6mm
Capacity	748cc
Comp. ratio	11:1
Claimed power	112bhp @ 11,000rpm
Carburation	4 × 35mm Keihin
Gearbox	6-speed
Tyres, front	120/70 × 17in
Rear	170/60 × 18in
Brakes, front	Twin 310mm (12.2in) discs
Rear	220mm (8.7in) disc
Suspension, front	Telescopic with adjustable compression and rebound damping
Rear	Pro-Link monoshock with adjustable preload, compression and rebound damping
Wheelbase	1,405mm (55½in)
Weight	185kg (407lb) dry
Fuel capacity	18 litres (4 gallons)
Top speed (approx.)	155mph (249kph)
Standing ¼-mile	12.2sec/120mph (193kph)

miniscule 1,405mm, with similarly racer-like steering geometry. The only disappointment was a price tag close to double that of its F-model sibling – and few who rode the RC30 doubted that it was worth every penny.

Light weight and brilliant handling gave the little bike the feel of a good 250, if not the RVF itself. The Honda's steering seemed so instant that it was as though the low clip-on handlebars were bolted straight to the 17in front wheel. Suspension was superb, and the front brakes unmatched on a roadgoing bike.

And the engine equalled them, at least when it was running properly, delivering even more of the traditional VFR's free-flowing power from tickover to well over 150mph (241kph) – and all the time with an evocative flat exhaust note from the 360-degree crankshaft V4. In town the radical riding position and monstrously tall first gear – good for over 80mph (130kph)! – made the Honda unbearable. On the right road it was simply supreme.

'Suddenly it all comes together: the road, the scenery, the feel of the bike, that droning exhaust,' I enthused in *Bike* before going heavily into debt to buy an RC. 'You're at Le Mans, powering onto the pit straight half a lap in the lead as the crowd prepares to invade the track at the end; or you're blasting towards the Waterworks having destroyed all opposition in the TT. On the RC30 you don't just compete in such races in your head – you win them all, too. The RVF always did.'

The RC30's introduction was not quite so smooth. A batch of race-kitted bikes embarrassed Honda by seizing in an important Australian production event, several racers had trouble with the titanium conrods, and several new types of valve were tried before unreliability was cured. But when they were running properly the RC30s were almost unbeatable on the track in 1988, and the arrival of Yamaha's even costlier rival, the FZR750R or OW01, a year later, failed to knock Honda off the top. In the 1989 Le Mans 24

The ELF Project: A Decade of Honda-Backed Innovation

When the VFR400R and RC30 were launched with their single-sided swing arms, the bikes became the first roadsters to make direct use of Honda's close involvement throughout the 1980s with the ELF racing team and their series of experimental chassis.

The project was born in the late 1970s around a Yamaha TZ750 two-stroke racing engine. It was the brainchild of Frenchman André de Cortanze, who as a leading Renault designer of the 1970s had been responsible for a Le Mans-winning race car and had worked on Renault's turbocharged Grand Prix car.

With some backing from the giant ELF petroleum company, De Cortanze set out to build a revolutionary motorcycle that did away with a conventional chassis and suspension completely, instead using a single arm bolted to each end of the engine assembly.

Initial development was slow but Honda quickly became interested, and provided factory 1,000cc RSC endurance engines for the 1980 season. De Cortanze's new bike, the ELFe, was low, light and very fast, but ironically unsuccessful in endurance events due mainly to the unreliability of its motors.

Honda's association continued when in 1984 the team switched to the high-profile world of Grands Prix. De Cortanze designed the ELF2 around factory-supplied RS500 two-stroke triple engines, later modifying the bike to produce the slightly less radical ELF2B first raced by Frenchman Christian Le Liard at the 1985 Le Mans Grand Prix.

When De Cortanze abandoned the project soon afterwards, ELF turned to the more pragmatic combination of race-team manager Serge Rosset and designer Dan Trema. Using Honda's works NS500 triple engine they produced the ELF3, which used De Cortanze's suspension ideas at the rear with a new front-end arrangement adopted from MacPherson strut car design.

In the hands of long-time Honda Grand Prix star Ron Haslam, this was the most successful ELF machine. Haslam scored the team's first world championship point in the bike's first race, the 1986 Spanish Grand Prix, and finished ninth in the championship that season. It looked as though ELF had finally made a breakthrough in motorcycle design.

By then Honda had begun investigating the possibility of roadgoing machines, and in 1987 they reached agreement with ELF to lease the necessary patents. But the triumphant arrival on the streets of the single-sided Pro-Arm system in 1987 was not matched by further success on the track. Centred on a more powerful works NSR500 V4 engine, the broadly similar ELF4 could never be made as fast as the conventionally chassised works NSRs. The hard-riding Haslam finished fourth in the championship in 1987 but his best results were gained on a standard factory NSR, before the ELF was completed.

The 1988 season saw another redesign to produce the ELF5, but three seventh places were the best that even Haslam could provide. By then François Guiter, the ELF marketing chief who had instigated the project with De Cortanze more than ten years earlier, was nearing retirement. At the end of the season the radical racer was abandoned.

Sadly for Honda, the Italian firm Bimota were set to beat the Japanese giant into production with a similarly radical bike called the Tesi, which was scheduled to hit the streets in 1991.

Hours, for example, five RC30s finished in the top ten behind the winning RVF and a handful of other factory bikes.

Most impressively of all, American Fred Merkel (Superbikes) and Englishman Carl Fogarty (Formula One) won back-to-back world championships in 1988 and 1989, taking four-stroke racing's most prestigious titles, against works opposition, riding RC30s fitted with race kits and some factory parts. Honda's roadgoing racer had been successful beyond the company's wildest dreams.

The RC30 was not the only V4 to be built with racetrack styling, a single-sided swing arm and a price inversely proportional to the bike's size and weight. Licensing laws mean that 400cc machines are very important in Japan, so for their domestic market the manufacturers produce scaled-down versions of many of the 600cc and 750cc bikes available elsewhere in the world.

Few other countries were treated to the original VFR400R, a delightful little bike with an alloy frame, Pro-Arm rear end, swoopy RC30-style full-fairing and a 398cc V4 engine that revved to 14,000rpm and produced a claimed maximum of 59bhp. It had much of the RC30's charm, a fair chunk of its speed, even less weight, and in Japan sold alongside straight-four rivals, including the similarly powerful CBR400F.

In 1989 the VFR was updated with the adoption of a 360-degree crankshaft in an even more compact engine. A beam frame, twin-headlamp fairing and even more power (to 63bhp at 12,500rpm) made the NC30, as the bike was code-named, a real mini-classic. A year later the NC30 surpris-ingly became available in Britain, but a price identical to the CBR1000's meant that only a few millionaires and dedicated hedonists bought one.

Designed in Deutschland: The ST1100

The most important new Honda of 1990 was also a V4, cost even more than the NC30, and was at totally the opposite

The ST1100 Pan European was designed by Honda's German headquarters to take on BMW in the fast-touring stakes.

ST1100 (1990)

Engine	Watercooled 16-valve DOHC 90-degree transverse V4
Bore × stroke	73 × 64.8mm
Capacity	1,084cc
Comp. ratio	10:1
Claimed power	100bhp @ 7,500rpm
Carburation	4 × 32mm CVs
Gearbox	5-speed
Tyres, front	110/80 × 18in
Rear	160/70 × 17in
Brakes, front	Twin 316mm (12.4in) discs
Rear	316mm (12.4in) disc
Suspension, front	Telescopic with TRAC anti-dive
Rear	Single shock with adjustable preload and rebound damping
Wheelbase	1,550mm (61in)
Weight	279kg (614lb)
Fuel capacity	29 litres (6.4 gallons)
Top speed (approx.)	135mph (217kph)
Standing ¼-mile	12.5sec/110mph (177kph)

Behind all the ST's plastic was a 1,084cc V4 whose cylinders, unlike the VFRs', were arranged across the frame.

end of the size and performance scale. The ST1100, known as the Pan European on one side of the Atlantic for its professed ability to transport its rider from one European capital to the next at speed and in comfort, was a sports tourer designed by Honda Germany to compete head-on with BMW.

The ST was a fully faired shaft-driven bike whose water-cooled 90-degree engine differed completely from previous Honda V4s by being placed across the frame rather than longitudinally. It was the company's first major new engine design since the CBRs of three years earlier.

The 1,084cc motor was a 360-degree unit; its sixteen valves opened via a bucket-and-shim arrangement. Toothed belts ran to a single large wheel on each side of the engine, from which the double overhead cams were turned by gears. Accessibility to the engine was helped by having the cylinder heads sticking outwards, as with a CX500.

Honda could doubtless have persuaded such a power-plant to produce more than 130bhp with plenty of torque, but instead limited the ST to a claimed 100bhp at 7,500rpm. This coincided not only with the maximum output of BMW's latest sixteen-valve four-cylinder engine but also with a voluntary horsepower limit for bikes sold in Germany. Honda were as aware of possible power-limit legislation as any manufacturer, as they had shown by initially declining to sell the RC30 and even the CBR1000 in America when political pressure was mounting in the late 1980s.

The new engine was used as a stressed member of a surprisingly old-fashioned steel twin-cradle frame. Though Honda made much of the ST's *sport*-touring capabilities, the bike weighed in at a hefty 614lb (279kg) even before the cavernous petrol tank below the rider's seat had been filled. Handling was predictably ponderous, and high speeds could trigger occasional wallowing even with the rear shock on its firmest settings.

The motor was the more impressive part of the package. Smooth, civilized and able to shoot the wide ST effortlessly up to almost 140mph (225kph), the V4 engine produced enough low-down and mid-range torque to make even previous Honda V4s seem positively peaky.

In the overall scheme of large-capacity motorcycles, the ST1100 fitted in somewhere between the Gold Wing and the CBR1000 as a long-distance roadburner. It combined the ability to cruise at twice most countries' legal limits with the comfort to do so all day, plus the fuel range that made it necessary to pause from doing so only after every 200 miles (320km). As such, the ST fulfilled its design brief – and was arguably the only bike on the market capable of doing so.

6

Best of the Rest

Oddball Models
through the Years

Two-Stroke Trespasser:
The NS400R

The first few bikes that Siochiro Honda built in the 1940s were two-strokes, but you'd never have thought so to judge from his company's output in later years. While Yamaha, Kawasaki and Suzuki produced hordes of screaming strokers, Honda stuck resolutely to four-stroke power for all but their smallest models.

Even the factory race effort was centred on a four-stroke, the infamous NR500, when Honda returned to the totally two-stroke-dominated Grands Prix in 1979. But after eventually finding success when Freddie Spencer won the world championship on the two-stroke NS500 in 1983, their first 500cc title, Honda finally brought out a roadgoing version in celebration two years later.

The NS400R looked just like the real thing, with fully faired racetrack styling, HRC (Honda Racing Corporation) stickers on the tailpiece, aerodynamic plastic shrouds covering the fork lowers and even the sidestand, and an aluminium alloy frame – Honda's first on a road bike.

Like the machine that inspired it, the NS400R was powered by a three-cylinder engine, its pots arranged in a 90-degree V3 formation. But rather than create a full-blown 500cc sportster to compete with the four-cylinder Yamaha RD500LC and Suzuki RG500 Gamma, Honda kept their race replica to only 387cc.

Honda optimistically claimed a maximum of 71bhp from the NS. The engine though was very peaky and the acceleration below 7,000rpm very poor, so fast riding required constant flicking through the six-speed gearbox. Top speed reached a disappointing 130mph (209kph) on a good day, and the crackly exhaust note compared feebly with that of the bike's raspier four-cylinder rivals.

The peaky, thirsty NS400R was no tourer, but the fine-handling two-stroke was an ideal bike for twisty highland roads.

But if the triple's engine was nothing special its handling certainly was. The alloy frame was stiff, the suspension at both ends was excellent, and the lightweight Honda's 16in front wheel and well chosen geometry meant it could be flicked around as easily as anything on two wheels.

As an all-round motorbike the NS400R was rather hopeless: expensive, thirsty (well under 30mpg if used

NS400R (1985)	
Engine	Watercooled 90-degree V3 two-stroke
Bore × stroke	57 × 50.6mm
Capacity	387cc
Comp. ratio	6.7:1
Claimed power	71bhp @ 9,500rpm
Carburation	3 × 26mm Keihin
Gearbox	6-speed
Tyres, front	100/90 × 16in
Rear	110/90 × 17in
Brakes, front	Twin 256mm (10in) discs
Rear	Single disc
Suspension, front	Telescopic with air-assistance and TRAC anti-dive
Rear	Pro-Link monoshock with adjustable preload
Wheelbase	1,385mm (54.5in)
Weight	163kg (359lb)
Fuel capacity	19 litres (4.2 gallons)
Top speed (approx.)	130mph (217kph)
Standing ¼-mile	13sec/105mph (169kph)

hard) and no quicker than humbler tackle such as Yamaha's RD350LC. But on a twisty back-road it had few equals. And few riders ever got off it without a smile on their face.

From about the same time Honda also produced a series of fast, peaky 125cc two-strokes, the NS and NSR125s, some of which were built at Honda Italia's plant in Atessa. The 1986 NS125 was a single-cylinder screamer which looked very similar to the NS400, produced 22bhp at 8,000rpm and had a top speed of about 70mph (113mph).

Its successor, the NSR125, was even more impressive. Now fitted with a genuine full fairing, it was styled to resemble the VFR750 – and the copy was so convincing that

The NS250 parallel twin and the later NSR250R V-twin were too expensive to sell well in most countries other than Japan.

at a glance the two bikes looked almost identical. Unfortunately, even Honda couldn't keep the illusion going once the two-stroke tiddler's tinny motor had crackled into life.

Naturally enough, in between the 125cc single and the 400cc triple came an NS250R twin, which was launched in 1984 and bore a close resemblance to the larger model. Excellent handling and 100mph (160kph)-plus performance went without saying but the parallel twin's high cost of construction ensured that it was rarely seen outside Japan, where lavishly equipped small-bore screamers remain hugely popular.

The even racier-looking NSR250R arrived in 1987, and was able to deliver a good portion of the performance suggested by its deliciously styled Grand Prix-replica bodywork and top-notch specification. Again, the price was high; few NSRs were seen outside Japan. But a handful of bikes escaped to be raced in the Isle of Man's production TT, and those who rode one knew they were on something a bit special.

The NSR's engine was a watercooled 90-degree V-twin, like that of the all-conquering NS250 on which Freddie Spencer had won half of his 250/500cc world championship double in 1985. The little roadster put out about 50bhp – good enough for over 115mph (185kph) – red-lined at 11,000rpm and weighed only 276lb (125kg) with fuel, thanks partly to a strong but light twin-spar aluminium frame.

On a sweeping road or a tight country lane, where the little bike's wailing exhaust note, adrenalin-pumping acceleration, flawless handling and brilliant braking overshadowed its peakiness and lack of comfort, the wonderfully evocative

NSR250R made every penny of its price seem worthwhile. If any bike could make you feel just like Freddie, this was the one.

Small Sales for Big Singles

Having progressed from one to two cylinders in 1957 in search of more revs and power, from then on Honda treated single-cylinder engines with little more enthusiasm than the company showed for two-strokes.

Like the strokers, the singles were initially built mainly with engines of 125cc or less. There were several dozen different small-bore four-stroke singles made during the 1960s and 1970s alone, none of them particularly memorable. Some were roadsters, typically designated CB or CD; others were dual-purpose trail bikes such as the SL and XL range.

Towards the end of the 1970s the biggest of these was still the XL350, which was launched in 1973 and combined 85mph (137kph) top speed with decent acceleration and fairly good handling both on road and off. Only the XL's tyres really failed to make the compromise, the shallow knobbles hampering grip on the street but proving almost useless in the dirt.

Various 185cc and 250cc versions followed, most of them fairly pleasant bikes if you didn't ask them too many questions off road, but the big step came in 1979 with the XL500S. This used balancer shafts to kill most of the vibration from an engine which made a claimed maximum of

The CB250RS of 1980 was quick, neat, nimble and reliable.

32bhp at 6,250rpm, and was good for a top speed of very nearly 100mph (160kph).

By 1982 the big XL had become even bigger, not in its single-cam motor (which remained at 498cc) but in its seat height, which grew by an ill-advised 1.5in to 34.5in – too tall to allow many riders to get a foot down with ease.

If the XL was good fun but a bit silly, the CB250RS single introduced in 1980 was just as enjoyable and also a very practical roadster. The RS consisted of a slightly modified four-valve XL250 motor – using a bigger carb, more compression and peakier valve timing than the current trail bike – in a sharply styled street chassis with a rectangular headlamp, single disc, twin pipes and vaguely Eurostyled lines.

With its 26bhp engine, good suspension and less than 300lb (136kg) of weight, the little RS was a remarkably quick and nimble bike. It would rumble up to about 90mph (145kph) without too much vibration, run for 60 miles (96km) on a gallon of petrol, and was as happy on the open road as it was when slicing through traffic or making use of its ample ground clearance in a tight bend.

Compared with Honda's rival CB250N Super Dream twin, the single was lighter, better-handling, almost as quick and much more handsome. It was also commendably cheap and reliable, although the engine's top end and the weedy final drive chain wore quickly. A little humble to be judged a classic, perhaps, but a very neat bike all the same.

Factory Customs: A Decade in the Limelight

The very phrase by which they became known is a contradiction in terms which hints at their supposed appeal. Hordes of high-handlebarred, stepped-seated, laid-back 'factory customs' were produced by all the Japanese companies in the early 1980s, most of them with huge V-twin engines. They were generally big, slow, heavy brutes, best suited to those who preferred admiring their reflection in shop windows to actual riding.

The V-cruisers, as they are more accurately described, were not so much custom bikes as variations on the theme perfected by Harley-Davidson, whose big V-twins have always held a unique appeal. Not unreasonably, when the Japanese firms saw Harleys selling at record levels in 1980 they decided to take a piece of the action.

Yamaha produced their Virago in 1981 and the other firms replied swiftly, Honda with a range of Shadows powered by 45-degree engines of up to 1,100cc. Later they built V4s called Magnas for the American market, too, with similarly laid-back looks and a little more performance – at least so long as you could hold on to those high bars and didn't plan on leaning too far round a corner.

In the early 1980s the cruisers were very popular in the States, taking much of Harley's traditional market. But the American company hit back in 1983 when they persuaded Ronald Reagan's government to put a heavy import tariff on motorcycles of over 700cc.

In following years the Japanese cruisers' sales were hit by the tariff and the strength of the yen, while Harley-Davidson took the opportunity to make vast improvements to their own bikes. By the time the tariff was lifted a few years later Harley was on the way to taking Honda America's number one spot in sales of large-capacity machines; by 1989 the Milwaukee firm had over half the domestic big-bike market to itself.

By this time, too, an increasing number of riders had decided that the big Japanese Vees lacked either the practicality of alternative oriental bikes or the charisma of genuine Harleys. The factory-custom following had faded. By the end of the decade the Honda VT1100 and its siblings had been cast back into the shadows.

The FT? No Comment

In 1982 Honda finally came up with the roadgoing big single that many people had been requesting for years. Or at least they produced the FT500, a roadgoing big single. Whether the FT was the bike that the enthusiasts had asked for was rather less certain.

Its motor was based heavily on the four-valve XT unit, merely substituting a new cylinder head and altering the

FT500 (1982)	
Engine	Aircooled SOHC 4-valve single
Bore × stroke	89 × 80mm
Capacity	498cc
Comp. ratio	8.6:1
Claimed power	35bhp @ 6,500rpm
Carburation	35mm Keihin
Gearbox	5-speed
Tyres, front	3.50 × 19in
Rear	4.25 × 18in
Brakes, front	300mm (11in) disc
Rear	300mm (11in) disc
Suspension, front	Telescopic with air-assistance
Rear	Twin shocks with adjustable preload
Wheelbase	1,435mm (56.5in)
Weight	174kg (388lb) wet
Fuel capacity	13 litres (2.9 gallons)
Top speed (approx.)	95mph (153kph)
Standing ¼-mile	15sec/85mph (137kph)

counterbalancers slightly in order to damp out vibration at a higher engine speed.

The bike was unfaired, with fairly high bars, and was styled to resemble an American flat-track racer (in the States the bike was called the Ascot, after a famous circuit). Its chassis was a combination of simple single-downtube frame, long-travel forks, twin rear shocks and single disc brake at each end.

The FT was tall but quite light, at well under 400lb (180kg). Despite rather soft suspension, and a tendency to

The flat track-styled FT500 – alongside a CB750F – was not very racy in its performance.

weave at speeds of much over 85mph (137kph), it handled pretty well. The brakes were powerful, the tyres broad and grippy and the Honda was good fun to throw about through slow and medium-speed bends.

The main problem was the supposed star of the show, its single-pot engine. Peak power was up a fraction to a claimed 35bhp but the Honda came nowhere near to delivering the great slugs of low-rev torque that a big single traditionally grunts out.

Performance at the top end was nothing to get excited about either. The weave at 85mph (153kph)-plus was rarely a problem because much of the time the FT refused to go much faster anyway. Top speed, at around 95mph (153kph), was inexplicably slightly lower than that of the trail bike XT. 'Floats like a butterfly, stings like a moth,' quipped *Motorcyclist*.

Not that the FT500 was a particularly bad motorcycle; it wasn't. It's just that, having waited all those years for Honda to build a big-single roadster, the thumper fans had hoped for something with a little more clout and charisma.

Single-Minded Tradition: The XBR500

The modern-looking FT500 was as much of a disappointment in the showroom as it was on the road, and Honda's next attempt at a big-single roadster took a different approach. The XBR500, which appeared in 1985, was styled with more sober lines which combined up-to-date

The XBR500 couldn't quite decide whether it was a modern machine of the 1980s or a throwback to the 1950s, but proved to be a very handy little motorbike.

engineering with a hint of the big old British bangers which had ruled the roads in the 1950s.

Its handlebars were low clip-ons, the tank was humped in shape, a plastic seat-hump covered the pillion seat. Finished in black, there was a definite hint of Velocette Venom. But elsewhere the Comstar wheels, big front disc brake, remote-reservoir shocks and twin silencers added a contrastingly modern look.

Happily, the XBR was much less mixed up than this visual

XBR500 (1985)

Engine	Aircooled SOHC 4-valve single
Bore × stroke	92 × 75mm
Capacity	498cc
Comp. ratio	9.2:1
Claimed power	44bhp @ 7,000rpm
Carburation	39mm Keihin
Gearbox	5-speed
Tyres, front	100/90 × 18in
Rear	110/90 × 18in
Brakes, front	300mm (11in) disc
Rear	Sls drum
Suspension, front	Telescopic
Rear	Twin shocks with adjustable preload
Wheelbase	1,400mm (55in)
Weight	176kg (392lb) wet
Fuel capacity	20 litres (4.4 gallons)
Top speed (approx.)	100mph (160kph)
Standing ¼-mile	14.5sec/90mph (145kph)

grunt up hills in a high gear, delivering a sledgehammer blow of combustion once every lamp post, or howl happily along up near the red-line like a racer.'

Performance was still not at all special by multi-cylinder standards, but the XBR would top the ton, and the leant-forward riding position meant that 85mph (137kph) cruising was as practical a proposition as on most unfaired machines. But even Honda's contra-rotating balancer shaft could not prevent vibration from numbing the rider's hands at sustained high speed.

If the single's looks held a hint of the traditional then so did its steering, which was slow and required a surprising amount of effort to make the relatively light bike change direction. At least the XBR was totally stable, though. And good suspension and brakes meant that it could be cornered with confidence.

The XBR sold only reasonably well in Britain, where a big-single's lack of speed and relatively high insurance cost, relative to smaller-capacity multis, is a major handicap. But Honda's thumper went down much better in Japan, where nostalgia led to the creation of versions with more obviously 1950s-inspired lines, and with names like the Clubman.

The rest of the world rarely got a look-in but in 1989 Americans were offered the GB500 single, which ironically was not for sale in Britain. This followed classic styling to the extent of having an even humpier petrol tank, painted in a classy hue somewhere between traditional black and British racing green, a single seat, spoked wheels and an unnecessary kickstart lever in addition to the electric foot.

As a mix of newish technology with classic style the little

cocktail might suggest. Three years of development had resulted in a maximum of 44bhp at 7,000rpm, a significant gain of 9bhp over the FT, from the more over-square motor (bore went up from 89 to 92mm; stroke down from 80 to 75mm) with its radial four-valve cylinder head.

Equally importantly, the new engine was much more flexible than the old, possessing what *Bike* described as a 'fabulously flat torque curve that can be used to make the gearbox feel obsolete on occasion . . . The XBR will either

Honda was a very reasonable compromise between engineering and marketing. Unfortunately, the American public was a little too hard-nosed to buy it. Many GB500s will probably still be gathering showroom dust in another thirty years' time.

While Honda's roadgoing single developed through the 1980s largely by becoming visually more old-fashioned, the company's trail thumper was instead made bigger, faster and flashier. First the XL500 was bored out to 591cc and given an XBR-type RFVC (Radial Four Valve Combustion chamber) cylinder head, the extra volume bringing claimed peak power to a similar 44bhp at a slightly lower 6,000rpm.

The XL600L, as the bike was known, made an attempt to cash in on the increasing cult following of the Paris–Dakar Rally, a 7,000-mile (11,500km), twenty-day race through the Sahara Desert which in the mid-1980s was producing ever-increasing amounts of death, glory and media hype.

A tiny twin-headlamp handlebar fairing and huge 6-gallon (27.3 litre) petrol tank hinted at Sahara-crossing ability with the aim of boosting sales, especially in France, where large trail bikes are traditionally very popular. But although the XL looked the part, it suffered even more than its predecessors from those old failings of excessive height and vague steering.

The single was further enlarged and developed in 1987 to produce the NX650 Dominator. This stretched the motor to 644cc, bolted it into a new chassis and added slick styling, incorporating a small frame-mounted fairing complete with vivid graphics across the sides. A flush-fitting front mudguard replaced the old XL's motocross-type affair.

Desert-race styling gave a purposeful appearance but you had to be brave, stupid or very tall to take the XL600R off-road.

The NX650 engine produced only one more horsepower at the top end, giving a total of 45bhp at 6,000rpm. But a new exhaust system, employing two separate pipes running all the way from the exhaust valves to a matching pair of silencers beneath the seat, gave a welcome boost to low and mid-range performance.

Automatics: No Gears, No Sale?

Many of Honda's best-selling models over the years have been small-capacity runabouts with no clutch or even gearshift to worry about – just a simple throttle and a couple of brakes, and a device to let the engine build up speed automatically.

But the company has also built some bigger automatic bikes, in an attempt to offer this convenience with more performance. The most notable was the CB750A of 1976, which used the faithful old four-cylinder motor, detuned by a lowered compression ratio (down from 9:1 to 7.7:1) to give only 47bhp at 7,500rpm instead of the normal 65bhp.

Changing between the two gears was still done by foot, which really made the 750 a semi-automatic. The automatic function was provided by a hydraulic torque converter, which worked like a clutch by driving oil through a pair of turbines, one driven by the engine, the other taking power to the rear wheel.

It was not the lack of tacho that gave the CB750A's game away, but the speedometer alongside: it was marked to show that the higher ratio, which was intended for speeds above 60mph (95kph), was geared for a top speed of 105mph (170kph). Not surprisingly, few riders were prepared to pay for that sort of performance along with the weight and bulk of a 750. The automatic was a flop.

Honda didn't give up completely, and in 1981 revealed an automatic version of their popular parallel twin, the CB400N. Again, the rider was spared the scuff marks on his left boot by a torque converter, though better acceleration was available if the lower of the two ratios was used for pulling away.

This time the motor was not detuned, but its transmission losses meant that the 400A was still left behind even by mediocre 250s.

The CN250 was an automatic which at least had the advantage of being purpose-designed for the job. Called the Helix in France, where it was sold before reaching Britain in 1990, the CN was a futuristic giant scooter, complete with luxuriously padded seat and a handy rear trunk.

Hidden beneath the fat seat was a 250cc watercooled four-stroke single engine that whirred the Helix gearlessly up to about 70mph (113kph). Comfortable, practical and even stylish, the CN made a useful commuter bike and was probably Honda's best automatic yet. But a high price – over 50 per cent up on the downmarket CD250 twin, for example – meant that it too was never likely to sell in big numbers.

Where the Dominator gained was in its usability. The suspension worked well on rough ground or smooth, helping the bike feel secure yet very flickable despite its big 21in-diameter front wheel. The frame-mounted fairing and flush-fitting front mudguard removed weight from the steering and at last got rid of the wind-generated speed weave with which previous models had been afflicted. And the seat was an inch lower at 34in – at least a small step in the right direction.

The heavily shrouded front disc was powerful and well backed up by the rear. Tyres were impressive, too, in nearly all situations. By the end of the 1980s several companies had come up with lightly treaded covers that were completely at home on tarmac, where most trail bikes spent the vast majority of their time, yet were also capable of delivering a decent amount of traction when the going got rough and conditions became more unfavourable.

Single-cylinder horsepower meant that the Dominator would never be a high-speed hotshot, of course. But it thundered up to a shade over 100mph (160kph), didn't

The single-speed CN250 – comfortable and stylish.

NX650 Dominator (1987)

Engine	Aircooled SOHC 4-valve single
Bore × stroke	100 × 82mm
Capacity	644cc
Comp. ratio	8.3:1
Claimed power	45bhp @ 6,000rpm
Carburation	40mm Keihin
Gearbox	5-speed
Tyres, front	90/90 × 21in
Rear	120/90 × 17in
Brakes, front	256mm (10in) disc
Rear	220mm (8.7in) disc
Suspension, front	Telescopic
Rear	Pro-Link monoshock with adjustable preload and damping
Wheelbase	1,435mm (56.5in)
Weight	152kg (334lb) dry
Fuel capacity	13 litres (2.8 gallons)
Top speed (approx.)	100mph (160kph)
Standing ¼-mile	14.5sec/90mph (145kph)

vibrate too badly and would have made a fairly handy long distance cruiser given a screen for its fairing and a petrol tank that held more than 3 gallons (13 litres). Combining nippy performance with light weight, good handling and sharp looks, even for the many owners who never ventured further off road than a pub car-park, it was arguably Honda's best and most enjoyable big single yet.

7

From Dream to Domination
How Honda's Racers Conquered
the World

Honda Enters, Honda Wins. The old advertising line is brilliant in its simplicity, outrageous in its arrogance, ruthless in its clarity. And, some might add, so smug it almost makes you want to spit. In recent years the top-level racetrack success of the world's biggest bike producer has been so frequent that many observers are glad to see Honda lose for a change.

Honda does lose sometimes, of course. In fact the company failed more often than it succeeded in its attempts to take road racing's 500cc world championship in the 1980s. Until Freddie Spencer's victory in 1983, Honda had consistently failed to land the crown despite spending millions of yen on two separate occasions in attempting to do so.

The huge corporation which often appears faceless and uniquely inscrutable has sometimes aimed too high, but the overall impression gained from a two-wheeled competition history that spans more than thirty years is one of Honda's unparalleled professionalism, dedication and engineering excellence.

And most of all the impression is one of success: of victory in race after race, championship after championship. The fact that 'Honda Enters, Honda Wins' rings true is proof that when Honda go racing, they simply do it better than everyone else.

Learning Fast, Revving High

As a former car racer of some note, Soichiro Honda was doubtless aware very early of the gains in prestige and technical knowledge that could result from testing his firm's products in competition. Even so, he was taking a bold step when in 1954 he combined a trip to view several European car plants with an exploratory visit to the Isle of Man TT races.

Soichiro had already declared that his firm would soon compete in the TT, and earlier that year had made his first foreign foray. A Honda-entered bike – two-speed 125 ridden by one Mikio Omura – finished thirteenth in an international race held to celebrate the 400th anniversary of the Brazilian city of Sâo Paulo.

At the time, the company was experiencing problems with the work-force in the aftermath of employing more than two thousand new workers to cope with demand for the successful Model-E Dream. Honda reasoned that the goal of foreign competition would raise staff morale, especially as national pride was still low less than ten years after the end of the war. But he received a shock when he reached the Isle of Man to find the potential opposition – German NSUs, Italian Guzzis and MVs – revving their engines far higher, making much more power and using far superior components to his own current machines.

On his return, Honda established a pattern for later years when he entrusted design of his race engine to a pair of young engineers – one of whom, Tadashi Kume, was to become president of the company almost thirty years later in 1983. To give such an important job to such inexperienced men was a gamble, but one which eventually paid off with the production of a competitive motor.

Before tackling the TT, Honda entered some domestic races during 1955, 1956 and 1957, winning a few, losing several more and learning much. On Soichiro's advice, the engine was made smaller and lighter. By TT time in June 1959, their 125cc twin, the RC142, was producing 16bhp at 14,000rpm – three times the output at twice the maximum revs of the E-model roadster of a few years earlier.

Having committed his team to going to the Isle of Man, Soichiro again set a pattern for the future by ensuring that the first attempt was made with a thoroughness that would

The Honda party arriving in the Isle of Man in 1959.

later become synonymous with Honda. Bill Hunt, a thirty-year-old American who was the General Sales Manager of American Honda – and who a year earlier had won a prestigious race at Mount Asama in Japan – was appointed rider and manager in a five-man TT effort.

Hunt went over to the Island several months before the event, sending back maps and films of the racetrack – which was not the famous 37.75-mile (60.75km) Mountain Circuit but the 10.8-mile (17.38km) Clypse course – to Japan for use by the other riders: Naomi Taniguchi, Teisuka Tanaka, and the inappropriately named and unrelated Junzo and Giichi Suzuki. The Honda party duly arrived, amusing unfamiliar Westerners by bringing their own cook, rice supply and mattresses for sleeping on the floor.

More laughs were provided by the team's knobbly tyres, better suited to ash-covered Asama back home. But these were soon swapped for Avons, and the local paper *TT Special* was impressed by the team's preparation: 'It was the workshops that caught our eye, with various white sheets on which, written in blue and red Japanese, were the names and numbers of all the other runners in the 125cc Lightweight event, race signals, course markings, and other information useful to the newcomer rider.'

The bikes were parallel twins, heavily based on the all-conquering NSU 250s with which Soichiro had been so taken in previous visits to Europe. The slightly inclined cylinders' twin overhead cams were worked by bevel gears. When the two-valve RC141 proved uncompetitive, more powerful four-valve RC142 cylinder heads were immediately flown over from Japan, adding yet more cost to an exercise which was estimated at over £10,000. That was more than some factories were spending on a whole season's racing in 1959, and was further proof of Honda's greater ambition of world domination.

The money was well spent, despite the fact that the Hondas could not stay near the MV Agustas of winner Tarquinio Provini or runner-up Luigi Taveri. Hunt crashed, but the four Japanese finished in sixth, seventh, eighth and eleventh places, with Taniguchi and the two Suzukis winning the manufacturers' team prize. As a debut this was undeniably impressive. Although the team did not stay in Europe to compete in the Grands Prix, few observers doubted that Honda would be back.

Storming Sixties: Honda's First Glory Years

The factory did indeed return the next season, complete with a twelve-man team, an improved 125 and also a formidable four-cylinder 250 racer that was made basically by doubling up the pots of the 125cc twin, whose over-square bore and stroke dimensions of 44 × 41mm were identical. This time Honda were more serious still, taking in six of the European classics as well as the TT, and signing the top-line Australians Tom Phillis and Bob Brown as well as several Japanese riders.

The bikes and riders were more competitive, although they still could not get anywhere near the MV Agusta factory's stars, Carlo Ubbiali and Gary Hocking. The Italian won both 125 and 250cc titles, as he had the year before, and meanwhile MV's John Surtees was equally dominant in the 350 and 500cc classes.

But Honda scored some good results, notably at the TT, where in the 250cc event Brown finished fourth ahead of Moto Kitano (also on a Honda) and Phillis, and where in the 125cc race Hondas swamped the places from sixth to tenth. And two things happened that year that would prove immeasurably important to Honda in years to come.

The first was that Jim Redman joined the team, after Phillis and Taniguchi had been injured. Redman had been poised to abandon hope of a works ride and go back home to Rhodesia (Zimbabwe) but he was immediately successful, finishing fourth in the 125cc Dutch TT and starting an association with Honda that would bring huge success to both.

The second was that MV shocked the racing world by announcing their retirement from the smaller classes at the end of the 1960 season, at the same time as Ubbiali and Surtees quit bike racing. How Honda would have fared the next year against the Italian factory was doubtless a subject of much debate among paddock-bar pundits at the time. No matter. MV were out and Honda were still in – and with an intensified effort that saw the factory put more bikes on the grid than ever before. For their official riders Honda stuck loyally to Redman and Phillis, although the reduced number of works seats had led to plenty of competition. 'You rode them when they were slow, so you can ride them now they're fast,' Soichiro was reported to have said. He also signed Swiss star Luigi Taveri from MV, and leased factory bikes to Bob McIntyre and the youthful Mike Hailwood,

Jim Redman: Captain Honda

The name Redman became synonymous with that of Honda in the early 1960s, when the previously little-known Rhodesian notched up six world championships and forty-six Grand Prix wins as team leader for the Japanese factory.

In the early days he had to ride particularly hard, and his speed on the less-than-competitive 125 and 250 machines in 1960 did much to put Honda on the map. When the factory came up with winning bikes he was repaid by being retained to ride them, and became known as an intelligent racer who could win while taking no unnecessary changes.

In 1962 and 1963 he took both the 250 and 350cc titles on Honda's fast-revving fours, retaining the bigger class for the next two seasons as well. Sometimes the Hondas' speed made winning relatively easy, though there was always a team-mate to beat. At other times he had to ride superbly, as when defeating Hailwood and his 350 MV Agusta for the first time in 1962.

Redman's career was ended when he crashed Honda's ill-handling 500cc four in 1966, and he went back home to Rhodesia – to import Yamahas.

whose father, Stan, secured the deal by arranging to sell Hondas in his chain of bike shops.

The result of all that was a near-total domination that was hard to believe at the time. Hondas won ten of the eleven 250cc Grands Prix and eight of the eleven 125cc rounds. Not only did Hailwood become 250cc world champion and Phillis win the 125cc crown, but at the end of the year

Luigi Taveri in the 125cc Isle of Man TT, heading
for the first of six straight victories that brought him
the 1962 world championship.

Hondas filled the first five positions in the 250 championship, plus five of the top six in the 125s. At the TT, Hondas were placed one to five in both races.

In fact Phillis was lucky with his championship, for the East German Ernst Degner was ahead on points after the penultimate Swedish round, when he defected to the West, leaving his championship chances along with his factory MZ behind the Iron Curtain. At the remaining Argentinian Grand Prix in Buenos Aires, Degner's borrowed EMC was uncompetitive and Phillis won the race and the title – only to suffer far worse luck himself when he was killed in the following year's TT.

For Soichiro Honda the 1961 season really must have been a dream come true, giving a return in terms of publicity and credibility that would have been unthinkable when those knobbly-tyred 125cc racers were unloaded in the Isle of Man just two years before. But in typical style he refused to stand still, attacking not only the 350cc world championship but also the new 50cc class in 1962.

There was little joy in the 50cc, where Taveri and his tiny eight-speed 10bhp bike could finish only third behind Degner, now riding for Suzuki. But in the other three classes the Hondas went from strength to strength, winning every round they contested to take the 125 and 250cc world championships with such ease that Suzuki and Yamaha withdrew to try and find more speed.

Taveri took the 125 title from Redman and Irishman Tommy Robb, who had signed for Honda at the start of the season. In the 125s, Redman won six of the nine races he contested to become champion ahead of team-mate McIntyre. And, more impressively, the Rhodesian took his 350 Honda – basically a bored-out version of the 250 four, producing around 50bhp at 14,000rpm from its 285cc engine – to a championship victory against not only Robb but also Mike Hailwood and mighty MV.

Redman was made Honda's number one rider, and he put his Isle of Man record straight the following year by winning both 250 and 350cc TTs on his way to another championship double. But 1963 was not such a successful season for a Honda team which had become used to winning: in the 50 and 125cc classes their bikes were outclassed by the Suzuki of New Zealander Hugh Anderson, who won both titles, and in the 250s not only did Morini rider Tarquinio Provini push Redman all the way, but Yamaha's Fumio Ito won the Belgian Grand Prix and promised a new challenge.

That threat materialized in a big way in 1964 when Yamaha, who like Suzuki had watched Honda's racing success pay dividends in the showrooms, signed Phil Read in an all-out bid for the 250cc world championship. Read's

Honda's world champion Jim Redman leads the Yamahas of Phil 'Foot-down' Read and Tommy Robb in the 250cc Ulster Grand Prix of 1964.

bike was a two-stroke twin; Redman's a new version of the four-cylinder four-stroke. Both riders and machines were so closely matched that the title race made great drama, often relegating the predictable 500cc event – Hailwood won all but one round on his MV – from top billing at the end of the day.

The best race was at Assen in Holland, where the two diced in boiling heat throughout the race, bashing legs and fairings as the lead changed six times in the last half-lap. Redman took it by a tenth of a second. He then increased his championship lead with second place in Belgium after his British rival's faster Yam had seized. But Read then put together three wins in a row to leave Redman needing victory in the final two Grands Prix of the season.

It was then that Honda chose to debut their secret weapon, the legendary six-cylinder 250, in an attempt to get more power and speed. The six was powerful and fast all right. It revved to 16,500rpm, put out 53bhp through its eight-speed gearbox, and ran to a top speed of almost 150mph (240kph). It was also completely untried in race conditions, although Redman had tested the bike in practice.

For a few laps of the Italian Grand Prix at Monza the gamble looked to have paid off. Redman howled into the lead and began to pull away – but then the six-pot motor began to overheat, and Read surged past to win the race and the world championship. Redman's easy victory in the 350cc championship, where he won every race, and Taveri's win in the 125s were scant consolation for Honda.

Things were even gloomier in 1965, when cars were becoming increasingly important to Honda and leaving less budget for bike racing. Read gave Yamaha a much easier win in the 250cc world championship. And, though Redman also retained his title, a young Italian called Giacomo Agostini, riding a three-cylinder MV Agusta which was slower than the Honda four but lighter and more nimble, made him work hard for it.

Honda also won the 50cc title, after four years of trying, when the tiny 23-year-old Irishman Ralph Bryans, riding an even tinier 20,000rpm-13bhp-100mph (160kph) twin, finally got the better of Anderson's Suzuki. But this season the 125cc four was outclassed to such an extent that Honda were provoked into unveiling one of their most exotic ever bikes for the end-of-season Japanese Grand Prix – an in-line *five-*cylinder 125 which was effectively two-and-a-half 50 engines joined together, the central exhaust pipe running up and over the engine before exiting to the right of the seat.

The five almost made a winning debut at Suzuka, where a broken cylinder-head bolt slowed Taveri to second place. But there was no mistake the next season, when the tiny Swiss won the world championship comfortably before Honda made the surprising decision to abandon the 125 and 50cc classes for the next season.

Honda's main news for 1966, though, was the signing of Mike Hailwood, who had won four easy 500cc championships on the trot for MV but was looking for a new challenge.

Hailwood was in a different class in the 250, taking the title by winning the first nine Grands Prix. And although Agostini gave him a hard time in the 350s the trusty Honda four was again good enough to win.

So might have been the awesomely fast 500, which revved to 12,000rpm, put out around 80bhp and screamed up to over 165mph (265kph). The 499cc four was supremely fast but terrible to ride, due to its poor handling. It worried even Mike the Bike at times, and proved an early example of Honda's tendency to regard engine development as more important than the chassis.

Even so, Honda's heavy horses might still have given them the 500cc title they wanted in 1966. Team politics determined that only Redman started the season on the 500, and after three rounds he led the championship from Agostini's MV. Then the Rhodesian crashed at Spa in

Mike Hailwood takes the 297cc Honda six to victory in the Junior TT of 1967, en route *to another world title.*

Mike Hailwood: Gentle Giant

A good part of Mike the Bike's brilliant career was spent racing *against* Hondas for the Italian MV factory, but many of his greatest victories came on the Japanese machines.

The good-natured son of a millionaire motorcycle dealer won his first world championship as a privateer, riding a loaned Honda in the 250cc class. Then he left to win four 500cc titles for MV, before racing's most glamorous star and its most ambitious factory finally came together.

After signing for Soichiro, Hailwood took the 250/350cc double with his usual flair in 1966 and 1967, but even he could not quite capture the 500cc crown that Honda so desired. Nobody could have given more, though, and his battles to tame the fearsome 500 are the stuff of legend.

Mike Hailwood was the man who had it all: supreme talent, boundless determination, great bravery (best illustrated when he dragged Clay Regazzoni from a blazing Grand Prix car in 1973, during a four-wheeled career that was only partially successful) and a modesty that endeared him to all who met him. His death in a car accident in 1981 shocked everyone in motor sport.

Hailwood just failed to win the 500cc title for Honda.

Belgium, breaking his arm so badly that the injury would eventually end his career.

A missed race, a crash and a breakdown had put Hailwood well down in the championship race, and though he came back strongly it was not enough. Bent valves put him out of the final Grand Prix at Monza, and Agostini won his home round to take the title by just six points.

The next year's 500cc battle between the two great riders was one of the hardest-fought of all time. For Hailwood it was just one part of the hectic 1967 campaign in which he was Honda's sole factory entry in the 250, 350 and 500cc classes. He later described it as the toughest season of his life, and after winning his third Dutch TT of the day at Assen, almost fell off the 500 at the end of the race through sheer exhaustion.

Luckily, Hailwood at least had things fairly easy in the 350 championship, where Honda enlarged the six-cylinder 250 to 297cc, giving it an extra 5bhp for a total of 65bhp at 17,000rpm. Hailwood won the first five rounds to take the title easily, but his 250 championship was a different story. The Honda ace tied on 50 points with Yamaha's Phil Read, winning only because he had scored five Grand Prix victories to Read's four.

The 500cc fight, incredibly, was closer still. Hailwood, who was unhappy with the four's handling, shared race wins with Agostini to keep the championship destiny alive until the last two rounds. Again it came down to Monza, where Hailwood had to win to stay in touch. In the Italian idol's back yard the Englishman put his Honda into the lead, shattered the lap record, pulled out a half-lap lead – and then, two laps from the flag, his bike stuck in top gear, letting Agostini breeze past to win.

For Hailwood there was only disappointment, and although he won the final Grand Prix in Canada it was not enough. Agostini finished second, retaining his world championship not on points, which were equal at forty-six each, nor even on race wins, of which they each had five. Agostini won because he had scored three second places to Hailwood's two.

The 500-four had failed by the narrowest of margins, its surplus of power unable to overcome the disadvantages of poor handling and unreliability. Sadly, the mighty machine would have no chance to redeem itself, for in February 1968 Honda announced that they were pulling out of Grands Prix completely to concentrate on car development.

In less than ten years Soichiro's people had come, seen and conquered all but the very pinnacle of motorcycle racing. Between 1961 and 1967 they had won sixteen world championships, 137 Grands Prix and set countless race and lap records. They had raised public awareness of the sport, given it a glamour and an image that had been missing before. But in the end, Honda had failed to land the biggest prize of all.

Returning the Hard Way: The Never-Ready NR500 Project

Honda had been out of Grand Prix bike racing for a whole decade when towards the end of 1977 they announced that they were planning a return to the 500cc fray. Naturally, being Honda, they would be using four-stroke power.

There was one very serious drawback to such a scheme. Throughout the 1960s the factory's success had been based round extracting healthy horsepower figures from four-stroke engines by using lots of tiny cylinders to give very efficient breathing. At the time of their withdrawal in 1967 there had been strong rumours that Mike Hailwood would be given not only a 500cc six for the coming season but a 250cc V8 as well.

But since then the rules had been changed. The 500 class was now restricted to four cylinders, and dominated by watercooled two-strokes, notably Barry Sheene's Suzuki and Kenny Roberts's Yamaha. A two-stroke motor makes twice as many power strokes per revolution as a four-stroke, so to match the opposition for horsepower Honda really needed to build an eight-cylinder engine.

Unable to do that, they attempted the next best thing and produced an eight-valves-per-cylinder V4. Because even Honda's designers couldn't cram eight valves into a conventional circular bore, they came up with a radical arrangement whereby the pistons and bores were shaped like a running track, with straight sides and semi-circular ends.

In theory it *was* almost a V8, with pairs of cylinders linked. End-to-end widths of 80 × 50mm, using a stroke of only 36mm, gave over 50 per cent more piston area than a conventional design of the same capacity. The aim was to boost intake efficiency to V8 levels, using large valve areas and plenty of revs. The V angle was 100 degrees, the double overhead cams were driven by gears, and there were two conrods and two tiny spark plugs per pot.

Not content with revolutionizing the internal combustion engine, Honda also chose the NR500 to try some radical chassis ideas. The frame was an aluminium monocoque, a single structure encircling the motor, which did not aid engine access. And the 16in wheels were the only ones in the paddock.

The NR500 was a bold concept containing much brilliant engineering, but this time Honda had bitten off even more than they and their millions of yen could chew. The first problem was the engine: despite all its advanced technology and a rev limit as high as 20,000rpm, the four-stroke could not be persuaded to make as much power as Suzuki's square-four or Yamaha's in-line two-strokes.

Honda did not ease their difficult task either, by taking on so much at once. The monocoque frame cracked repeatedly, illustrating the designers' inexperience in the use of aluminium, and the small wheels gave more problems. When the NR was first tried in 1979, riders Mick Grant and Takazumi Katayama, the Japanese star, were running Dunlop and Michelin rubber respectively. Both companies had to build special tyres from scratch.

World-wide interest in the new bike was enormous, which only served to increase Honda's embarrassment when its long-awaited debut ended in spectacular failure.

Rider Mick Grant and race team manager Gerald Davison manage to smile despite their problems with the NR500 in 1979.

The Grand Prix team was based in Slough, west of London, and the NR was billed to appear at the 1979 British Grand Prix at Silverstone.

As the race approached, the team knew that the machine would be nowhere near competitive. 'It was compact but not light – like a lump of lead,' Grant would later admit. 'I remember following a 250 Yamaha in open practice at Silverstone, and it was slowly pulling away from me on the straight. I couldn't believe it.'

Spencer at the 1985 Italian Grand Prix in Mugello.

They bravely decided to go ahead nevertheless, and both Katayama and Grant scraped in at the back of the grid in qualifying. But the worst was yet to come. When the pack of two-strokes screamed away at the start of the 500cc Grand Prix, neither Honda left the line. A few seconds later

Freddie Spencer: Fast but Flawed

It would be sad if Frederick Burdette Spencer were remembered more for his later performances than for the ones that went before. Since 1986 he has become a figure of fun best known for his numerous ailments, repeated no-shows and occasional disappointing rides when unfit.

Freddie was always a difficult man to fathom – a deeply religious, intensely private individual from Louisiana in the Deep South of America, whose reserve seemed strangely at odds with the bustle of a Grand Prix paddock.

Spencer's background was typically American: racing at the age of six, a mini-bike champion by nine. By the time he signed for Honda at seventeen he had years of dirt-track success behind him. He won the firm their first 500cc championship in 1983, and two years later became the first rider to lift both 250 and 500cc titles in the same season.

But it was the way Fast Freddie brought a new dimension to the science of controlling a motorcycle which made him special. Kenny Roberts had pioneered rear-wheel steering but Spencer alone was comfortable with his front tyre, too, skidding sideways across the track. Sitting coolly above an out-of-shape NSR500 is surely how Freddie Spencer should be remembered.

Katayama was off, droning round the first corner. Then Grant appeared, unaware that his bike had sprung an oil leak.

As the Yorkshireman came to the first bend in a solitary last place, the oil on his back tyre tipped him off and the incalculably expensive NR500 burst into flames. Grant was uninjured but not so Honda's pride. And the company's humiliation was complete when Katayama pulled in after only a handful of slow laps.

The NR500 – whose nickname 'Nearly Ready' was gradually adapted to 'Never Ready' – did improve considerably during the next couple of seasons. British chassis expert Ron Williams was brought in to advise on the project, and simplified matters to good effect with a conventional tubular steel frame and 18in wheels. The cylinder angle was reduced to 90 degrees, and a one-way partial-slip clutch was adopted to mask the motor's disconcerting tendency to stop almost dead when the throttle was shut.

By 1981 the NR was quick enough for Freddie Spencer, Honda's fast-rising star, to qualify it ahead of Kenny Roberts's Yamaha for a non-championship meeting at Laguna Seca, California. By then the motor had been redesigned more than once, but it was still not reliable at ultra-high revs and failed to complete the race.

Back at Silverstone for that year's British Grand Prix, Spencer knew that he had to keep the revs well below the 22,000rpm limit to have much chance of finishing. Freddie wasn't having any of that, though, and screamed it up to fifth place before the inevitable blow-up.

The NR had failed yet again, but at least it had gone out with some pride. When the project was finally abandoned at the end of the season, the NR500 had cost Honda many millions of pounds, several years of probable racetrack success and a good chunk of their near-unbeatable reputation.

The V4 road bikes would soon be launched, owing much to the NR experience, and an oval-pistoned NR750 roadster looks set to make its debut in the early 1990s. But the price of that knowledge had been a high one indeed.

Two-Stroke Triumph: The NS500 Triple

Having drawn an expensive blank with one radical design, Honda might have been expected to retaliate with something very conventional when they finally resorted to two-stroke power in 1982. Not a bit of it.

Both Yamaha and Suzuki started the season with refined versions of the engine layout that had taken Italian Marco Lucchinelli to the previous year's championship on a Suzuki RG500: a square four, with induction controlled by disc valves. (Unlike the alternative reed valves, which are opened by engine suction as the mixture is drawn into the combustion chamber, disc valves turn with the crankshaft and open at precise times, then allowing the mixture an uninhibited path.)

By the second Grand Prix of the season, Yamaha would give Kenny Roberts a brand new V4, also with disc-valve induction. But Honda, surprisingly, turned instead to a reed-valve engine with only three cylinders, arranged in a

110-degree V formation with two pots almost upright and the other pointing forward.

The NS was the brainwave of an engineer called Shinichi Miyokoshi, who had been responsible for some of Honda's successful single-cylinder motocross motors, and the triple owed much to their design. Its single crankshaft gave an advantage in reduced friction over the rival fours, which were in effect two geared-together twins, and although slightly less powerful – around 125bhp, against the fours' 135 – the Honda engine was lighter and more compact.

Even so, few observers gave it much chance against the fearsome fours. Roberto Gallina, manager of the Italian Suzuki team, was quoted as saying that Lucchinelli would not even be able to qualify the NS, after Honda's fat wallet had prised the champion and his number one plate away from the Suzuki set-up.

The opening Grand Prix in Argentina was a revelation. Honda didn't win, but Freddie Spencer tagged on to a race-long battle between Yamaha-mounted Roberts and Sheene to finish a close third. Behind him, Lucchinelli and Takazumi Katayama, the latter delighted to be rewarded with a fast bike after his years of toil on the NR500, finished fifth and sixth respectively.

By the Dutch TT in June, traditionally the season's halfway point, Honda were getting closer still. At Assen they unveiled an aluminium frame, replacing the original steel tubes, and a carbon-fibre swing arm that saved even more ounces. New exhausts gave more power, but Freddie crashed in the rain and Katayama could finish only ninth.

Eight days later, appropriately enough on Independence Day, 4 July, Fast Freddie made amends round the flowing curves of the Belgian Grand Prix at Spa-Francorchamps. After Kenny Roberts's much more powerful V4 Yamaha had slowed, its rear tyre falling apart under the strain, the twenty-year-old Spencer took the lead and pulled away to take his first Grand Prix win and Honda's first for fifteen years.

It was a momentous occasion for Spencer and his employers, summed up by the sight of the ecstatic winner toppling over as he tried to turn round after crossing the finishing line. Everyone knew it was unlikely to be the last victory for either. Freddie managed only one more that year, as Italian Franco Uncini put in some consistently strong rides to win the title for Suzuki, but by the start of 1983 the precocious Spencer and Honda were a formidable combination.

The season turned out to be one of the great road-racing confrontations of all time, as Roberts and Spencer fought it out right down to the wire. The two Americans were as different as their Japanese machines: Roberts the wisecracking old master trying for a fourth title on his tyre-smokingly potent Yamaha four; Spencer the shy young pretender aiming for his first championship on the nimble Honda triple.

Spencer and Honda took first blood, running off three straight wins while Roberts's new OW70 Yamaha was slowed or stopped by overheating, a split exhaust and then by running out of fuel. Roberts clawed some points back at Germany's Hockenheim, winning while Freddie slumped to fourth with a split pipe of his own.

At Jarama in Spain, Spencer got the better of a race-long

Spencer at Spa, leading Raymond Roche, Kenny Roberts and Barry Sheene en route *to his first Grand Prix victory (1982). Even Freddie couldn't always win with his eyes shut, but sometimes it seemed that way.*

*Duel in the San Marino sun – Spencer shadows
Kenny Roberts at the final Grand Prix of 1983,
heading for second place and Honda's first 500cc
world championship.*

dice with Roberts which illustrated just how evenly matched the two men and their machines really were. 'That was the hardest race of my life,' said the exhausted boy from Shreveport afterwards. 'That was the hardest I've seen somebody ride to beat me,' echoed Roberts, who was to

have reason to revise that statement before the season's end.

In Austria the Honda's crankshaft snapped, and the victorious Kenny was back in the hunt. Spencer won again in Yugoslavia, where Roberts could finish only fourth after getting away dead last, but from the next race onwards the Yamaha seemed to have the edge. While Freddie began to suffer from front tyre trouble, the legendary triple champion they called King Kenny came back into the running, winning three races out of three to close to only two points behind with two races left.

Next was Sweden, where the pair again became locked in a fearsome struggle far away at the head of the field. The race – the whole world championship – was decided two bends from the end, in a manoeuvre that stunned even the battle-scarred Roberts, and which left nobody in any doubt that his quiet young rival from the Bible Belt possessed a chillingly intense will to win.

Roberts, his Yamaha the faster bike, had led onto the Anderstorp airfield circuit's long straight for the last time but had been forced to shut off momentarily by an involuntary wheelie. Spencer, seizing his chance, had kept with him down the straight and then come out of the slipstream to outbrake Kenny on the inside. But Roberts had seen him and released the brakes to pull fractionally ahead as they shed speed into the bend.

And then fearless Freddie had also released his brakes, surging forward and putting the two men onto the dirt at the outside of the track. 'Spencer went berserk. He ran me off the track and I don't think he realised just what might have happened,' said the disgruntled Roberts later, after his rival had recovered first to take the vital win.

Berserk it might have been – but the incident had all but won Freddie the title. A month later, in the season's final Grand Prix at Imola in Italy, Spencer needed to finish only second to claim the crown.

Roberts alternately led and then followed Spencer in a desperate attempt to slow him down, while Eddie Lawson on the second Marlboro Yamaha tried equally desperately to catch Spencer and give his team-mate the points advantage he needed. But, in front of 100,000 spectators and a world-wide television audience of millions, Freddie Spencer and his Erv-Kanemoto-prepared NS500 withstood the pressure, took second place and finally won the 500cc world championship that Honda had been chasing for so long.

In Search of More: The NSR500 V4

The triple had been a brilliant success, all the more praiseworthy because of the way its design had challenged – in a fashion not normally associated with Honda – the accepted thinking that high horsepower figures were all-important in Grand Prix racing. But Roberts's results on the latest V4 Yamaha in the latter part of 1983 had made it obvious that even Spencer would struggle to make up the triple's power deficit a year later.

Honda needed a V4 of their own, and by the start of the 1984 season they had one in the shape of the NSR500. Like their own triple but unlike the Yamaha, the NSR motor had only one crankshaft and was thus a true 'V' rather than a geared-together 'W' in shape. The cylinders were positioned at 90 degrees, fitted with ATAC chambers which varied exhaust volume with engine speed (as on the NS500 and the NS400 roadster), and induction was by reed valves opening into the crankcase.

So far, so good: the four immediately made more peak power than the triple, around 140bhp, and Honda looked set for another winning season. Even after Spencer's practice crash at the opening round in South Africa, caused by a collapsed carbon-fibre rear wheel, the prospects were bright. Without the retired Roberts to worry about, Freddie won the next round at Italy's Misano from Yamaha's new number one, Lawson.

But the confidence in the NSR had been misplaced, the bike's failings disguised by Misano's tight corners. It soon became clear that Honda had tried to do too much with the new machine, almost as they had with the NR500 four-stroke. The NSR's chassis featured a twin-spar frame of pressed aluminium, which was no great problem, but in an attempt to lower the centre of gravity the fuel tank had been placed below the engine, with the exhaust pipes replacing it on top.

Not only did the arrangement give carburation problems due to hot intake air and also the need to remove the painfully hot pipes for access, but Freddie found the upside-down layout detrimental to the bike's handling. He described the NSR as 'like having a heavy rock on the end of a long stick; very difficult to control', and proved the point by crashing heavily in a non-championship race at Donington Park.

The NSR was never really satisfactory during 1984, remaining as difficult to steer as it was fast in a straight line, but Spencer might still have taken the title. He switched back and forwards between the four and the faithful old triple, winning on both during the course of the season – in Germany on the NS, in faster France and in Yugoslavia on the NSR.

But Spencer then took another non-championship tumble, this time breaking a shoulder when he ran out of brakes at Laguna Seca in California, and in his rival's absence Steady Eddie cruised to the title on his Yamaha.

Smokes and Fire:
The Rothmans Connection

For Honda the 1984 season had been little short of disastrous, but the year ended on a very positive note. Over Christmas Honda signed a multi-million-pound sponsorship deal with cigarette giant Rothmans, which would stretch into the next decade.

The cash, which was initially estimated at between £3 million and £5 million spread over two years, was undoubtedly useful to Honda in running their increasingly expensive Grand Prix team. But even such a sum made up only a small part of the factory race budget, and Honda's somewhat surprising decision to swallow corporate pride and paint their bikes in another firm's colours went far beyond instant finance.

'We did it not for the money but because we knew Rothmans had promotional skills that we could not equal,' explained Honda Racing Corporation director Takeo Fukui, who set up the deal. 'Rothmans can promote motorcycle racing to a much wider audience.'

The truth of that was soon apparent in the huge 'Honda City' of motorhomes, transporters and hospitality units that became a central feature of Grand Prix paddocks, dwarfing even affluent rivals such as Marlboro Yamaha. The Rothmans deal brought bike racing – and particularly Honda – into the big league of sponsored sports and escalated a Grand Prix tobacco war that would dominate racing for many years.

The American Randy Mamola, who had ridden well on a factory triple in 1984, joined Spencer as a full member of the Rothmans-backed HRC team for the 1985 season, as did long-serving Honda man Takazumi Katayama. Britain's Ron Haslam and Australian Wayne Gardner also wore navy-blue-and-white leathers, riding as a Honda Britain squad.

But there was no doubt about who was number one. While the others rode NS500 triples, only Freddie was provided with a pair of new NSR500 V4s, now completely redesigned with a new twin-spar aluminium frame and with its exhausts and fuel tank back in their normal positions. Not only that but Spencer had a brand-new 250 too. Honda already had a production 250cc V-twin, the RS250R, but the new NS250RW was nothing like that. It was effectively half the NSR V4, sharing the same 54×54mm dimensions, its V angled further forward like the four's. Power output was around 75bhp.

Freddie originally planned only to contest a few Grands Prix on the 250, but was so impressed with the bike in pre-season testing that he decided to have a shot at the championship. The other riders in what had previously been a supremely close and hard-fought class soon wished he hadn't bothered, for Spencer and his bike were both in a league of their own. In the first nine rounds he failed only twice and often won seemingly at will, dicing with the Yamaha pair Carlos Lavado and Martin Wimmer and with the Honda-mounted German veteran Anton Mang before speeding up to clear off over the horizon at half-distance. By the British Grand Prix, at soggy Silverstone in August, he could afford to splash to the title with fourth place.

The 500cc battle was proving much harder. Honda's V4 made more power than Yamaha's twin-crank engine, but it was not without its faults. The single crankshaft made the engine wider, and also created a gyroscopic effect which made the bike feel cumbersome in corners. Even without that problem, the 145bhp motor was more than a match for its hard-pressed chassis and tyres. A real Honda.

Ron Haslam: Fast on Everything

The young lion they called Rocket Ron made his name in the 1970s on a TZ750 Yamaha, and the wise old hand headed towards the end of his career in the 1990s on an Italian Cagiva, after a spell with Suzuki. In between times the quietly spoken, universally popular man from the Nottinghamshire village of Langley Mill spent the best years of his career on Hondas.

He never won a major world championship, or even a Grand Prix – though he made the rostrum many times, and would almost certainly have taken the 1985 South African Grand Prix had not his NS500 seized and thrown him off. But Haslam probably won more races on more different types of Honda motorcycle than anyone.

The two world championships he did win both came shortly after he joined the Japanese factory: the Formula One title in 1979 was followed by his Formula Three victory a year later. Countless wins on four-stroke race bikes were followed by triumphs on the CB1100R street bike, then by more wins on two-strokes.

Many thought that Honda held Haslam back in Britain for too long, wasting his hungriest years. But when he did try Grands Prix Ron often led them, and he finished equal fourth in his best season of 1985. The next year Ron rode the radical ELF, and on it earned an unequalled reputation as a development rider.

Honda men Randy Mamola, Wayne Gardner and Ron Haslam get their heads down in pursuit of eventual winner Spencer at the Belgian Grand Prix in 1985.

Until 1985, 250cc Grand Prix racing had been a nail-biting, close affair. Freddie and his Honda V-twin added a new dimension to win seven of the first nine rounds.

The NSR500 was not quite right when it appeared in 1984, but it was still fast enough for Spencer to be able to show off its four exhausts while winning the French Grand Prix.

Spencer in the Le Mans sunshine while mechanics prepare a bike for practice.

Although the NSR's handling was improved in mid-season by moving the engine forward in the frame, Spencer still preferred the feel of the triple and would almost certainly have returned to it for some rounds had Honda politics allowed. As it was, he did try the NS briefly in practice for Le Mans. But Spencer won on the V4 that weekend, just as he did in seven of the ten Grands Prix that he finished on it during the season. While the NSR was fast yet still flawed,

Freddie celebrates after wrapping up his 1985 double
championship with a 500cc win in Sweden.
Third finisher Ron Haslam looks on admiringly
while, in the background, Eddie Lawson reflects
that he is now an ex-champion.

its rider was just Fast Freddie – arguably the most talented motorcycle racer of all time, and at the age of twenty three at the peak of his powers.

Freddie could probably have won on almost anything, and he could certainly win on the NSR500, which often seemed to slither and squirm under impossible cornering and acceleration forces as Spencer sat calmly on top of it under complete control. He secured his second 500cc title in Sweden with a fourth straight win – and then sparked a situation that would become depressingly familiar in the seasons to come.

Although his bikes, mechanics and crew arrived for the final race in Italy, Spencer was nowhere to be seen. Instead, the new double champion despatched a spokesman to announce that he had reinjured a crash-damaged thumb in the gym. Spencer was staying at home, and Rothmans' champagne stayed in its bottles.

There was rather less celebrating in the Honda camp during a 1986 season that went wrong even before the word go. Spencer failed to turn up for pre-season testing in Brazil and for the traditional year-opening meeting at Daytona in Florida, blaming sinus trouble. Nor did he attend a test session in Yugoslavia – but, being Freddie, he still put the Mk III NSR on pole for the opening Spanish Grand Prix, then took the lead in the race and began to pull away.

But from about the tenth lap of that fateful day, 4 May 1986, it was all downhill for Freddie Spencer. His right forearm began to pump up with tendinitis from the pressure of using the front brake, and he was forced to slow his pace and then retire. Nobody dreamt it at the time, but the world had already seen the best of the young genius, whose forearm operation meant he would not score a point all season.

Spencer's absence let in Wayne Gardner, who had been rewarded with an NSR after finishing equal fourth in the championship with his Honda Britain team-mate Ron Haslam, a year earlier. Gardner benefited initially, winning his first Grand Prix in Spain after Spencer had pulled in. But the pressure of suddenly becoming Honda's number one was something the young Australian could have done without.

Instead of enjoying a gentle learning year, he found him-self the only Honda rider with a realistic chance of the championship – and, ironically, the first-race win only made matters worse. 'I didn't like it at all,' he later admitted. 'The Honda guys kept telling me not to let the situation worry me but everybody knew the pressure was there. There are 200 people at Honda Racing Corporation whose only purpose is to produce a bike that wins the world championship . . . and all their efforts were riding with me.'

Wayne Gardner: Mr Hundred Per Cent

A stocky Australian whose natural friendliness sometimes slips to reveal a short temper, Gardner earned the 'Hundred Per Cent' nickname in Japan with a string of victories at Honda's home track at Suzuka. The tag could justifiably be used to describe a fierce determination which is outstanding even in the competitive world of Grand Prix racing.

Wayne is a battler, which sometimes gets him into trouble. Another nickname is the Wollongong Wild One, and Gardner's aggressive rear-wheel-spinning riding – coupled with bad luck – saw him throw away his world championship chances with heavy crashes in 1989 and 1990.

But when he stays on board Gardner is a formidable force. He arrived in England for the 1981 season and within a year had been signed up to begin a long association with Honda. In 1984, a clutch of British domestic titles to his name, he paid his own way into some Grands Prix and took a third place in Sweden.

The next season he was a fully paid up factory star; a year after that, in Spencer's absence, he was Honda's top gun. Gardner finally reached his goal of the world championship in 1987, and his skill in taming an unruly NSR500 shone even in defeat a year later. Injuries have since hit him hard, but Gardner's determination means he will surely be back.

Wayne Gardner, known for his own brand of Aussie grit and rear-wheel sliding technique.

Gardner also came up against another big problem. Unlike Spencer, who was always happiest when revving a fierce motor right off the clock, Gardner had been brought up on four-strokes and preferred a more gentle power delivery. While the Aussie fought a 153bhp engine that kicked viciously at 11,000rpm and sent the back tyre scrabbling sideways, Eddie Lawson found his more tractable Yamaha easier to ride and just as quick.

Even worse, the slow-starting Gardner was hit from behind on the starting grid at Monza, bashing his knee on the NSR's footrest. After losing a lap in the pits for repairs he could finish only sixteenth behind the victorious Lawson, who then hit form to reel off four straight wins and take a big lead in the championship race.

Gardner won at Assen, where the American fell, and at Silverstone, where the Australian conquered the cold and rain with characteristic belligerence. But most of the year Lawson and his YZR500 Yamaha were simply too fast and too consistent. Eddie rode better than ever, and made very few mistakes indeed.

In the 250cc class, too, Honda lost to their biggest rivals despite producing 'Spencer Replica' NS250RWs for half-a-dozen favoured riders. The Spaniard Sito Pons finished second in the championship, the Frenchman Dominique Sarron was third, the German Anton Mang fourth and the Frenchman Jean-François Baldé fifth. But the veteran Yamaha star, Carlos Lavado – exciting if a little error-prone – beat them all to take the title on a Yamaha that for most of the season was a faster bike than all the Hondas.

Honda's approach in the 250cc class was similar in 1987,

when they again supplied works V-twins to six European riders. This time the result was very different: the revised NSR Hondas were generally quicker than the five factory Yamahas, and made a clean sweep of a thrillingly tightly contested championship. When the dust cleared, old man Toni Mang had ridden faster and especially harder than anyone else. The German won his fifth world title ahead of his compatriot Reinhold Roth, Pons, Sarron and the Spaniard Carlos Cardus.

And in the 500cc class it was another hard charger, the increasingly confident Wayne Gardner, who took the honours for Honda. Again, much was expected of the returning Freddie Spencer. This time Fragile Freddie missed the first

By 1987 Gardner was ready, and so was the Honda NSR500.

race, his shoulder injured in a pre-season crash at Daytona. He returned for the third round in Germany only to suffer a freak accident when a plastic protector left a deep cut in his knee, and further disasters with lost contact lenses and lost enthusiasm meant that Spencer scored only four points all year.

The season was all about Gardner, who like the NSR had in a year matured from an also-ran to the dominant force in the championship. Twelve months earlier he had been wishing Spencer would return to take some pressure off; now the Australian welcomed the absence that allowed Honda's effort to be centred on him. Twelve months earlier he had found the bike verging on unridable; now it had been redesigned to suit him rather than Spencer.

The cylinders were opened up to 112 degrees, allowing the carbs to be more efficiently placed in the centre of the V and facilitating an improved exhaust design. The ATAC system was dumped in favour of a Yamaha-style exhaust power valve which varied the height of the exhaust port, and helped give much more mid-range power.

Handling was also improved, with a new chassis and also by reversing the direction of crankshaft rotation. Most importantly, the 160bhp NSR was decidedly quicker than the opposition. 'Every time I see a Yamaha I wait for a straight and blast past, just to remind them how I felt last year,' an exultant Gardner said at the fourth round in Italy, where he again beat Lawson to extend his championship lead.

Gardner won six of the first eleven rounds, ignoring a nosebleed in Italy and pain from a practice-crash injury in Yugoslavia, and when he didn't win he was nearly always

second or third. He clinched the title with an overwhelming start-to-finish victory at Goiania in Brazil. Honda were back on top of the world.

Honda didn't exactly rest on their laurels before the 1988 season – the NSR was completely revised yet again – but unfortunately for them the changes did not work. The engine was again made more compact, and its comparatively broad power band compressed to find some extra top-end urge. Coupled with a new chassis whose lengthened swing arm put more weight on the front wheel – the opposite of what Gardner claimed he'd requested – the 1988 NSR's sudden rush of power meant that the champion struggled to find traction coming out of corners.

By round four in Jerez it was obvious that even Gardner's hard riding could not tame the bucking, sliding, head-shaking NSR500. 'I don't enjoy riding any more because it has got me scared,' he admitted before struggling to fifth place. 'We have tried everything possible in the way of suspension adjustment and nothing makes any difference.'

Worse, Gardner then crashed and broke his foot while testing a new frame. But the modifications had worked, and the NSR was a much better bike. Although Gardner struggled to eighth in the German rain, by round seven in Austria he knew he could beat Eddie Lawson and perhaps even pull back a twenty-point deficit.

He might have done so, too, but at the peak of a head-to-head battle between the two men around the fearsome Salzburgring, Wayne's NSR suddenly seized, tipping him off and letting Eddie stroll on to win and double his advantage.

'I guess I can say goodbye to the championship now,' said

Joey Dunlop, five times Formula One world champion, with bike-mounted camera on the Isle of Man.

Island master Dunlop had time to stop and remove a loose silencer yet still win on his RS750 V4 in the 1984 Formula One TT.

the Australian, and he was right – though not before Yamaha had been given a fight. Gardner won the next three races, then in France looked to have got the better of a thrilling race-long four-way dice with Suzuki's Kevin Schwantz, local ace Christian Sarron and the injured Lawson.

But, cruelly, on the last lap the NSR seized again. Lawson won, and two rounds later the ultimate professional finished second behind Gardner to win back the title with a race in hand.

Honda's disappointment in the fallibility of their 500 was partially avenged in 250cc class, where the latest version of the NSR250 again proved good enough to take four of the

Joey Dunlop: Master of the Roads

Honda's V4 four-stroke was in many ways the most successful race bike of the 1980s, dominating championship after world championship in the Formula One and Endurance classes. Nobody had more success on the growling RS and RVF than Joey Dunlop.

Joey was a wonderful enigma. Small and almost painfully shy, his often scruffy appearance and near-impenetrable Irish accent hid a razor-sharp mind that would visualize every nut and bolt of a factory V4 motor – never mind every patch of tarmac on his beloved Isle of Man TT course.

On the open spaces of a man-made racetrack Dunlop was just another useful racer, but on the roads of the Island and his native Ireland he was for years almost unbeatable. His first TT success came on a Yamaha in 1980. At the end of the season he signed for Honda, and in 1982 the man from Ballymoney took the first of five consecutive Formula One world championships.

It was ironic that, having escaped serious injury during a long career Joey should come close to retirement after badly breaking a leg at Brands Hatch in 1989. A year later he returned to the TT hoping to match Mike Hailwood's record of fourteen wins, but a disappointing week showed that the old form proved hard to recapture.

first five places. Spaniard Sito Pons beat his Yamaha-mounted compatriot Juan Garriga to take the championship, after a year in which his smooth yet rapid style had rarely seen him finish outside the top three.

But things didn't go quite so according to plan in the 125cc class, newly limited to single-cylinder machines. Honda still declined to build a full-works bike, but instead supported two riders – Italian star Ezio Gianola and the previous year's third-place man, Hans Spaan from the Netherlands. The pair received special HRC engines which produced over 40bhp at 12,500rpm, complete with more mid-range power than any of their rivals. But the Honda's chassis was unchanged and crude by comparison: a twin-spar aluminium frame with simple cantilever rear suspension set-up.

Handling was poor in comparison with that of the JJ-Cobas ridden by the talented teenage Spaniard Alex Criville. At only nineteen, Criville proved he could outride even the best 125cc men in the world, and his speed was matched by a cool resistance to pressure. He won the last two Grands Prix to take the title in style.

Sito Pons had a much less stressful time in retaining his 250cc world championship, despite having not only three Yamahas but no fewer than seven factory Hondas in opposition. Sito's machine did receive a little extra help from HRC, sometimes gaining an edge with new parts before the other Honda men had a chance to try them. But for the most part it was the Spaniard's fast, intelligent riding that put him out in front. He wrapped up the title at Donington Park with three rounds still to go.

Champion Eddie Lawson's defection from Yamaha to Honda over the winter had stunned the racing world – not least Wayne Gardner, who was less than happy to find himself only joint number one. As it happened, the Aussie need not have worried. A week after an inspired victory in his first ever home Grand Prix at Phillip Island, Gardner crashed at Laguna Seca and broke his leg badly enough to end his championship challenge in round three.

Wayne Rainey, riding for Kenny Roberts's Lucky-Strike-sponsored Yamaha team, won in America and proceeded to score top-three finishes with supreme consistency to emerge as favourite for the crown. But all the while Steady Eddie Lawson, who had started the season in pain from an injured wrist, had been attempting with his team manager Erv Kanemoto to improve the latest NSR500. Before the

Eddie Lawson and the NSR500 in 1989. With Erv Kanemoto's help, he knocked the unruly Honda into a championship-winning machine inside a season.

season, the engine had been modified yet again to give a more forgiving power band. But, although fast, the Honda

Erv Kanemoto: Star in the Shadows

Although he invariably declines to take any credit, preferring to stand in the background while his riders enjoy the spoils of victory, Erv Kanemoto made a uniquely vital contribution to most of Honda's Grand Prix success in the 1980s.

The large, mild-mannered Californian with the oriental features was instrumental not only in Freddie Spencer's championship wins in 1983 and 1985 but also in Eddie Lawson's title in 1989. Team manager, tuner and arguably the most knowledgeable man in a Grand Prix paddock, since 1982 he has been the Honda factory's closest link with the racing world.

In his early days Kanemoto prepared Yamahas for riders including Gary Nixon and Barry Sheene, but it was with the precocious Freddie Spencer that he became associated most closely. Freddie was always quick to pay tribute to his friend and mentor's almost telepathic understanding of what needed to be done to his bikes – which made Spencer's later habit of leaving Kanemoto awaiting his arrival all the more mystifying.

After Spencer's departure Erv found only partial success with Niall Mackenzie as his rider, but in 1989 HRC gave him the chance to set up his own team with Eddie Lawson. The manner in which the duo turned a wayward NSR500 into a championship-winning machine illustrated the exceptional skills of both men.

In the 1970s the American Russ Collins put three highly-tuned CB750 motors in a row to make this frighteningly fast drag racer.

Dave Thorpe, three times winner of the motocross world championship.

Honda continues to take up new challenges

Motocross was another sport that Honda entered and came to dominate. Britain's Graham Noyce won the factory's first 500cc world championship in 1979, and in the 1980s Honda took charge. The Belgian André Malherbe won in 1981 and 1982, and his compatriots Georges Jobé and Eric Geboers repeated the feat in 1987 and 1988. Most successful of all was Britain's Dave Thorpe, who took the title in 1985, retained it a year later, then came back to win a third championship in 1989 before leaving to ride for Kawasaki.

Honda proved they could build trials bikes, too, in the early 1980s. The Belgian Eddie Lejeune routinely performed impossible stunts to take a hat-trick of world championships in 1982, 1983 and 1984.

did not much like changing direction. Kanemoto and Lawson worked ceaselessly through the early part of the season, altering handling by changing the engine position and by bracing the aluminium frame. Lawson struggled on the track but consistent second and third places kept him in the hunt.

By Le Mans, round eleven, the Honda was ready. Lawson won fair and square, then finished second to Kevin Schwantz at Donington to close within five points of Rainey. In Sweden the pressure was on, and Rainey, until now so consistent, made a crucial mistake. Planning an overtaking move to get past Lawson's faster Honda, he lost concentration and crashed. Eddie took the win, and with two rounds left was in control.

French ace Jean-Claude Chemarin and his co-rider Christian Leon led Honda's endurance-race effort in the 1970s.

Chemarin's four-cylinder RCB endurance bike formed the basis for roadsters such as the CB900FZ.

A couple of second places were enough to bring Lawson his fourth world championship. It was his first for Honda, after being a thorn in their flesh for years, and in many ways his hardest-won crown of all.

But Honda's joy turned to frustration when the champ signed for Kenny Roberts, taking his number one plate back to Yamaha. Once again the pendulum had swung, although it would be Lawson's Team Marlboro compatriots who spoiled Honda's 1990 season.

Both Eddie and Wayne Gardner had their challenges wrecked by leg injuries that forced them to miss vital rounds. Suzuki's main hope, Kevin Schwantz, again threw away his chance with crashes, which allowed the supremely consistent Wayne Rainey to lead the championship race from start to finish.

In the 250cc class Honda's works NSR was again the fastest bike, but Yamaha had the quickest rider. After a season-long battle with NSR-mounted Carlos Cardus, brash 22-year-old John Kocinski took the title with a last-round victory in Australia.

8

The Three Rs

Running, Riding and
Restoring

Defining a 'classic' motorcycle is something that no two enthusiasts seem able to agree on, but most would accept that the interest in old motorcycles, which has grown so quickly around British bikes in the last decade, has more recently spread to include early Japanese machines too. Some traditionalists still hate them, but Japanese classics are on the way up.

Not only important Honda models such as the CB750 and the CB450, but even more recent bikes such as the original Gold Wing and the CB400/4 are increasingly being bought and restored to their former glory by nostalgic individuals who remember them the first time round, or at least remember their good points. So too are the rarer, smaller models from the 1960s – the C72 and CB72, the CB92, and many of the humbler twins and singles.

Some can be bought and ridden immediately; others require complete stripping and rebuilding. For some people,

reconstructing an old bike is more fun than riding it. But, before embarking on such a project for the first time, be sure that you have the ability and resources – including the time and patience – to finish it. The job may take much longer and cost far more than you think.

Acquiring one of these older bikes is a much more specialized business than merely buying a more modern model, because there are fewer examples on the market and the majority will require at least some attention. It is possible to buy through magazines, both the weekly newspaper *Motor Cycle News* and the numerous specialist classic bike publications, but for older Hondas one other avenue is through clubs – either the Honda Owners' Club, whose British branch is due to have a separate classic section by the time this book is published, or the Vintage Japanese Motorcycle Club.

The latter is an organization formed in America in 1979 to

cater for enthusiasts of Japanese bikes of more than fifteen years old. There are now branches in Britain and Australia, too, and predictably Hondas are well represented. Not only does the British branch freely dispense advice which could be invaluable to anyone contemplating a restoration project, but they welcome members who do not own a bike but are interested in buying one. The club magazine includes numerous advertisements for bikes and bits.

Prices of old Hondas have not yet become ridiculous in the way that those of certain British bikes have, but machines in really good ('concourse', to use the classic buffs' jargon) condition are not cheap. At the 1990 Classic Bike Show in Staffordshire a fully restored 250cc CB72 from the early 1960s was auctioned to a museum for close to £4,000 – approximately the price of a new CBR600.

A restored original CB750 would be worth just as much, although a slightly later model in less than perfect condition would perhaps fetch only half that figure. Prices are changing all the time, but in general they are going up. Even later models are benefiting. The six-cylinder CBX1000, increasingly regarded as a classic although too young for the VJMC, has risen in value in recent years, thanks largely to nostalgia.

Buying an older bike offers the opportunity to choose from a fully restored masterpiece to a selection of rusty lumps of metal in a box. Basket-cases can be useful as a source of spares for the main project, but as the basis of a complete bike should be avoided. Many vital and expensive bits will almost certainly be missing; and, in addition, stripping the bike down gives an invaluable opportunity to discover where all the parts go and what extras are needed.

Best bet is to buy as complete a bike as possible, and this is even more true for novice restorers. Paying extra for a machine whose basics – notably the engine, suspension, petrol tank, seat and mudguards – are in good condition will make life easier and save much more cash later.

Before attacking the bike, a would-be restorer is advised to acquire a few basics for the job. Access to a clean, dry, well lit workshop is one necessity, as is a decent metric tool-kit and preferably a vice. No special tools are needed

Graham Blunden of the VJMC with his restored CB750, CB72 and CB450 Black Bomber.

for most early Hondas, although the official clutch-holders, bearing-pullers and valve-spring-compressors all make life easier. An impact-driver is handy for removing the special soft-compound cross-headed engine screws.

Honda's early workshop manuals are generally of little use, many of them being written in a strange Japanese/English, but the parts books contain detailed exploded diagrams and also the factory numbers of the parts themselves, and are very handy. Being able to quote part numbers is a big help when ordering spares.

Copies can occasionally be found at classic autojumbles, which are advertised in the classic magazines, although the emphasis of such events is heavily British. A few bike shops, such as Mead Speed from Newport Pagnell in Buckinghamshire, also carry a selection. The most comprehensive source in Britain is Dave Ayesthorpe of the VJMC, who will provide photocopies of virtually any model's manual for a small charge.

Armed with that lot, you're all set. Most restorers advise tackling the engine first, because if a motor is stripped to reveal horrendous damage it might make the whole project a financial non-starter. It's better to find out sooner than later. If a rebuild is viable, the common approach is to complete it and then store the lump away before starting on the chassis.

When it comes to putting the bike back together, the good news for Honda restorers is that virtually all the parts are still available, even for the earliest models. This is in marked contrast to the situation with Yamaha, who will supply very few early parts at all, and gives Honda a big advantage over Suzuki, Kawasaki and Bridgestone, the other Japanese marques of the 1960s.

Armed with a part number, it is theoretically possible to order even the earliest bits from any Honda dealer. In practice some dealers are much more helpful than others (contact VJMC or see the Useful Addresses list). Supply might take anything from a week to as long as six months, if a part is not in stock at Honda's European spares headquarters in Ghent in Belgium, but it will almost certainly turn up eventually. Further good news is that it will probably fit and work; quality control is better than for most old British parts.

The bad news is that such spares are expensive, which is not really surprising. Parts for 1960s Hondas cost 1990s prices, roughly similar to similar bits for current models, so ordering a long list of new parts including major items such as tanks and exhaust systems can bring the cost of a rebuild to more than the eventual value of the bike. If you have enough time, gradually picking up parts second-hand from small ads will save a great deal of money.

One other drawback of 'new-old' Honda spares is that they are not all exactly as originally supplied. Although the factory are prepared to make a run of parts for old models, they compromise a little by producing bits that will do for several models. Cables of slightly different lengths and colours are resupplied identical to each other; tank badges for some of the early 250s are made in metal instead of the original plastic.

Such details are only apparent to the real fanatics, and fortunately most VJMC experts seem refreshingly free from the stuck-up attitudes sometimes found in classic circles – although a rebuild will come under very close scrutiny if brought to a club run or function, where any faults will be ruthlessly exposed. A further benefit of the VJMC is that some of the few parts unavailable from Honda – early footrest rubbers and even the huge alloy nuts holding the handlebars of the CZ50 monkey bike, for example – are being made in small batches by enthusiastic members.

Club experts will also normally be happy to recommend good firms to supply the services – such as chrome and zinc plating, beadblasting and alloy polishing – that will be necessary to complete a thorough rebuild. Some enthusiasts have collections of a dozen or more old Hondas, all immaculately restored, and have experienced the disappointment of entrusting an important job to a company whose work turns out to be substandard.

Paint finish is another area where advice can be valuable. Most early Honda paint will long ago have lost its original colour (the basic red turns orange with time) but there is a consensus on some common shades – Ford's Sunset Red is a good match for the Honda shade used on early twins, for example. It is also sometimes possible to get a colour-match from an area that has been hidden under a tank badge or similar, and to get paint mixed to suit.

For those who are keen and knowledgeable enough, restoring an old Honda can be very rewarding, but for some owners the dream of an immaculate CB72 turns into expensive frustration instead. If you own an old Honda and don't want to restore it yourself, one option is to trust the job to a professional.

Some unobtainable parts such as the handlebar nuts of the CZ50 monkey bike are made in small numbers by keen restorers.

Although paying someone else to do the work is less satisfying and more expensive than doing it yourself (and will probably cost more than simply buying a completed bike in the first place), an experienced restorer will be able to save some money by repairing bits that might otherwise be junked, by having or knowing where to find second-hand parts, and by combining several damaged components to make one good one. Get a quote on the price before committing yourself, if at all possible.

Even when a restoration is completed, getting the bike

on the road might not be straightforward. If a vehicle has not been registered (and doesn't therefore have a Form V5) in Britain since 1983, when the Swansea DVLC was computerized, then it will be given a Q plate to signify an unknown date of manufacture unless you can provide suitable evidence about its background.

Given a photograph of the bike and a photocopy of the old-style logbook, both the Honda Owners' Club and the Vintage Japanese Motorcycle Club are normally happy to supply Swansea with a letter of accreditation regarding the model's age and rarity. The DVLC should then allocate an age-related registration number – not the bike's original number, but at least one that will look right when displayed in white-on-black lettering on the front mudguard.

Another very necessary piece of paper is an insurance certificate. If you already ride a bike, it's possible that an additional machine will be covered under a rider policy, or can be added to an existing policy at little extra expense. If not, or if the insurance company treats each bike as a totally separate

Autojumbles can be a useful source of cheap parts, but most are geared towards British bikes.

Honda's parts manuals are very detailed and useful for restorations. They can sometimes be found at autojumbles (above) or be obtained through clubs such as the HOC or VJMC.

item, you'll probably save money by insuring an old machine through one of the firms specializing in classic-bike cover.

These tend to be smaller operations, many of which offer very competitive agreed-value cover for restored machines – which would otherwise be rated only as typically worn-out second-hand bikes by an insurer. The owner normally has to provide photographs of the shining specimen, possibly with receipts to prove it has been rebuilt, or with a valuation by a third party such as a specialist dealer or owners' organization. Some insurers insist on the owner being a member of a recognized bike club.

There are generally strict limits to the ages of riders and machines covered: typically fifteen years minimum for the bike, twenty-five for the rider. Some firms limit the annual mileage, or increase premiums above a certain figure; some have a sliding scale whereby the premium is a fixed percentage of the agreed value of the machine. Some deal only in fully comprehensive policies – but even so premiums are often much cheaper than what the insurance giants charge for just third party, fire and theft cover.

Reduced-rate cover against fire and theft can also be arranged for bikes that are not being used on the road, for example while under restoration. Finding the type of cover best suited to an individual's needs requires a fair bit of phoning around for quotes, but the time will probably prove well spent.

Any motorbike of over three years old will also require an MOT certificate, which lasts for a year and involves passing a test covering brakes, lights, steering, exhaust, tyres and horn.

The engine is a good place to start a restoration, because if it is too badly damaged the job might not be worth continuing. Parts are still available for motors such as this 250cc CB72 unit, and crankshafts can be repaired if damaged.

Old machines create extra problems of their own, through such potential hazards as frayed brake cables, dodgy electrical connections, tyres that are cracked with age, and generally loose nuts, bolts and spokes. If a bike is used infrequently, it's important to give it a quick check-over before riding – particularly tyre pressures, cables and electrics.

*Immaculate restored bikes such as this CB450 Black
Bomber can be worth several thousand pounds.*

If a motorcycle is stored for more than a month or two its
battery should be removed and given an occasional trickle
charge, exposed metal should be treated to a thin coat of
grease or WD40, the fuel tank and carbs should be drained
of petrol, the engine should be turned over every so often
to keep its innards coated with oil (or the oil drained, spark
plugs removed and pistons given an occasional squirt of oil),
and the tyres should be deflated a touch and raised off the
ground.

But Soichiro Honda didn't build all those bikes to be stored
away in some grotty garage. If you are fortunate enough to
own one of the fifty million-plus motorcycles that have been
manufactured with those all-important five letters on the
tank since Soichiro sat on the floor drinking sake and dream-
ing his Dreams in 1949, don't waste the old man's inspiration.

Polish your Honda, rebuild it, customize it, show it off,
read about it and dream about it yourself if you must. But,
best of all, get out on the road and *ride* it!

Useful Addresses

Clubs and Associations

CB750 SOHC Owners' Association
836 Spruce Street
Alton
Illinois 62002
United States

Gold Wing European Federation
Trevor White
Gummenholzweg 4
CH 3173 Oberwangen
Switzerland
Tel: (031) 340 881

Gold Wing Owners' Club of Great Britain
Dave Horner
18 Arncliffe Way
Cottingham
North Humberside HU16 5DH
United Kingdom
Tel: (0482) 847307

Gold Wing Road Riders' Association
P.O. Box 14350
Phoenix
Arizona 85063
United States

Gold Wing Touring Association
Bud Morris
2322 S. Rogers 36
Mesa
Arizona 85202
United States
Tel: (602) 820 9584

Honda Owners' Club
Dave Barton
18 Embley Close
Carmore
Nr Southampton SO4 3QX
United Kingdom
Tel: (0703) 869301

Honda Sport Touring Association
9310 167th Avenue
Redmond
Washington 98052-3739
United States

International CBX Owners' Association
American branch
Clint Hooper
1603 City View Drive
Wichita Falls
Texas
United States
Tel: (817) 855 6977

British branch
Peter Broad
57 Osborne Close
Basingstoke
Hampshire RG21 2TS
United Kingdom
Tel: (0256) 465329

Australian branch
Michael Coppolino
PO Box 335
Mermaid Beach
Queensland 4218
Australia
Tel: (075) 529 074

Vintage Japanese Motorcycle Club
Canadian branch
John Armstrong
18 Stephanie Avenue
Nepean
Ontario K2E 7A9
Canada

British branch
Don Leeson
29 Bishop Road
Bollington
Nr Macclesfield
Cheshire SK10 5NX
United Kingdom
Tel: (0625) 574440

Australian branch
Grant Douglas
PO Box 499
Broken Hill
New South Wales 2880
Australia
Tel: (080) 883 377

Racing Clubs

American Historic Racing Motorcycle Association
265 Morris Street
Morgantown
West Virginia 26505
United States

Canadian Vintage Motorcycle Group
Jim Moore
250 Satok Cr
TH32
Milton
Ontario L9T-3P4
Canada

Classic Racing Motorcycle Club
Ann Murden
Fenn Farm
St Mary's Hoo
Rochester
Kent ME3 8QY
United Kingdom

Forgotten Era Racing Club
Jeff Miller
36 Farndon Road
Sutton-in-Ashfield
Nottinghamshire NG17 5HT
United Kingdom

Historic Racing Register
Peter Scott
44 Ravel Street
Seven Hills
NSW 2147
Australia
Tel: (02) 624 1262

Spares Specialists

Dave Ayesthorpe
1 Penarth Way
Aston on Carrant
Tewkesbury
Gloucestershire GL20 8HL
United Kingdom
Tel: (0684) 72862

Frettons of Coventry Ltd
House of Honda
Bishop Street
Coventry
West Midlands CV1 1HU
United Kingdom
Tel: (0203) 228227

P. F. K. Ling Ltd
136 St Peters Street
Lowestoft
Suffolk NR32 1UD
United Kingdom
Tel: (0502) 573758

Rex Judd Ltd
415 Burnt Oak Broadway
Edgware HA8 5AH
United Kingdom
Tel: (081) 952 6911

Tippets Motors (Surbiton) Ltd
312–320 Ewell Road
Tolworth
Surbiton
Surrey KT6 7AW
United Kingdom
Tel: (081) 399 2417

Professional Restorers

Peter Rhodes (Honda Specialist)
Unit 2
Culraven Yard
Haigh Road
Haigh
Wigan
Lancashire
United Kingdom

Steve Tonkin Restorations
18 Main Road
Bolton-Le-Sands
Carnforth
Lancashire LA5 8DH
United Kingdom
Tel: (0524) 823729

Specialist Classic Insurance Firms

Badbury Insurance
13 Salisbury Street
Blandford Forum
Dorset
United Kingdom
Tel: (0258) 455660

Bain Clarkson Ltd
PO Box 27
Falcon House
The Minories
Dudley
West Midlands DY2 8PF
United Kingdom
Tel: (0384) 455011

Carole Nash Insurance
19 Mayfield Road
Timperley
Altrincham
Cheshire WA14 7TB
United Kingdom
Tel: (061) 980 1305

D. & J. Davies (Brokers) Ltd
11 North Bridge Street
Shefford
Beds SG17 5AW
United Kingdom
Tel: (0462) 813030

Footman James & Co. Ltd
Waterfall Lane
Cradley Heath
Warley
West Midlands B64 6PU
United Kingdom
Tel: (021) 561 4196

Chater and Scott Ltd
8 South Street
Isleworth
Middlesex TW7 7BG
United Kingdom
Tel: (081) 568 9750

Hill House Books
The Mill House
Eastville
Boston
Lincolnshire PE22 8LS
United Kingdom
Tel: (020 584) 377

Motor Books
33 St Martin's Court
London WC2N 4AL
United Kingdom
Tel: (071) 836 5376

Specialist Booksellers

Bruce Main-Smith Retail Ltd
PO Box 20
Leatherhead
Surrey KT22 8HI
United Kingdom
Tel: (0372) 375615

Bibliography

Collecting, Restoring and Riding Classic Motor Cycles, by Tim Holmes and Rebekka Smith (Patrick Stephens)

Cycle World on Honda: 1962–1967, 1968–1971, 1971–1974 (three volumes) (Brooklands Books)

Fast Bikes: The New Generation, by Colin Schiller (Osprey)

Honda: An American Success Story, by Robert L. Shook (Prentice-Hall)

Honda CB750 (sohc), by Peter Shoemark (Haynes)

Honda: The Early Classic Motorcycles, by Roy Bacon (Osprey)

Honda Gold Wing: An American Japanese Motorcycle, by Peter Rae (Motorbikes International)

Honda: The Man and His Machines, by Sol Sanders (Charles E. Tuttle)

Honda Motor: The Men, the Management, the Machines, by Tetsuo Sakiya (Kodansha International)

The Illustrated Encyclopedia of Motorcycles, by Erwin Tragatsch (New Burlington Books)

Japanese Motorcycles: The Machines and the Men behind Them, by Cyril Ayton (Frederick Muller)

Motorcycles, by Charles E. Deane (Sundial Publications)

The Pictorial History of Motorcycling, by Tony Middlehurst (Magna Books)

The Story of Honda Motor Cycles, by Peter Carrick (Patrick Stephens)

Racing Books

Fast Freddie, by Nick Harris and Peter Clifford (Motor Racing Publications)

Kimberley's Grand Prix Bike Team Guide: Honda, by Michael Scott (Kimberley's)

Motocourse (Hazleton Publishing) (annual)

Motorcycle Grand Prix Year, by Michael Scott (Scott Books) (annual)

Ride It! The Complete Book of Endurance Racing, by John Robinson (Haynes)

Road Racers Revealed, by Alan Cathcart (Osprey)

The Wayne Gardner Story, by Nick Hartgerink (Fairfax Magazines)

Index